Unfree Labour Relations in Brazil's Amazon Region. An Assessment of the Changes Due to the Political Crisis Under the Bolsonaro-Government

Joseph C. Miller Memorial Lecture Series

eds. Janico Albrecht, Jeannine Bischoff, Sarah Dusend

Volume 26

UNIVERSITÄT BONN

BONN CENTER FOR DEPENDENCY AND SLAVERY STUDIES

Julia Harnoncourt

Unfree Labour Relations in Brazil's Amazon Region. An Assessment of the Changes Due to the Political Crisis Under the Bolsonaro-Government

ebv BERLIN

EBVERLAG

Bibliographic information published by Deutsche Nationalbibliothek
Die Deutsche Nationalbibliothek lists this publication in the Deutsche Nationalbibliografie; detailed bibliographic data are available at [http://dnb.ddb.de].

Gefördert durch die Deutsche Forschungsgemeinschaft (DFG) im Rahmen der Exzellenzstrategie des Bundes und der Länder – Exzellenzcluster Bonn Center for Dependency and Slavery Studies (BCDSS) EXC 2036/1-2020, Projektnummer: 390683433

Funded by the Deutsche Forschungsgemeinschaft (DFG, German Research Foundation) under Germany's Excellence Strategy – Cluster of Excellence Bonn Center for Dependency and Slavery Studies (BCDSS) EXC 2036/1-2020, Project No.: 390683433

Cover | Layout: Rainer Kuhl

ISBN: 978-3-86893-488-5

Internet: www.ebverlag.de
E-Mail: post@ebverlag.de

Printed in Germany

Introduction

Trabalho escravo, a form of unfree labour, has been considered a crime under Brazilian law since 1995. In 2023, Brazilian labour inspectors freed more than 3,000 labourers from this labour condition, which is the highest number since 2009. In total, the Amazonian state of Pará still bears the highest number of labourers freed from *trabalho escravo*. In comparison to the other states, however, it is going down in the ranking.[1] Why exactly this is happening is unclear even to people fighting locally against this form of labour exploitation.

This article deals with the changes in the system of *trabalho escravo* in Pará after the coup against Dilma Rousseff in 2016. As *trabalho escravo* is an illegal form of labour relation, a lot of elements remain unknown. But still there are data on and accounts from labourers who have been freed from this labour relation. Due to the danger encountered by the labourers in this situation, it is very difficult to do interviews with them, as attested to by Ricardo Rezende Figueira in 2004, who worked in the field as a priest and human rights activist for many years.[2] Interviews with the perpetrators are even harder to get and are dangerous as well. This is why this study is based on two series of interviews with experts working in the field, those freeing and supporting labourers who had been subjected to *trabalho escravo*, such as judges, lawyers, members of social groups, and labour inspectors, for example. In 2014, when I interviewed the militant members of the landless movement (*Movimento sem Terra*/MST) – a leftist grassroots movement that squats on the agricultural properties of enterprises that had broken the law, for example, by using *trabalho escravo* – I was also able to interview one labourer who

1 Welton Máximo, "Brasil resgatou 3,1 mil trabalhadores escravizados em 2023: Apesar de falta de fiscais, essa é a maior marca anual desde 2009," Agencia Brasil, 03.01.2024, https://agenciabrasil.ebc.com.br/direitos-humanos/noticia/2024-01/brasil-resgatou-31-mil-trabalhadores-escravizados-em-2023 [accessed 09.02.2024]; SmartLab, "Observatório da Erradicação do Trabalho Escravo e do Tráfico de Pessoas," https://smartlabbr.org/trabalhoescravo/ [accessed 09.02.2024].

2 Ricardo Rezende Figueira, *Pisando fora da própria sombra: A escravidão por dívida no Brasil contemporâneo* (Rio de Janeiro: Civilização Brasileira, 2004): 26, 28–29.

had been subjected to such labour conditions. This was during the first interview series, which was conducted in the second half of 2014. The second interview series was mainly carried out in autumn 2022. This time gap between the two series allows for an analysis of the changes that transpired before and after the coup against Dilma Rousseff of the labour party (PT) in 2016. Apart from the interviews and secondary literature, this study is also informed by official statistics, the so-called "dirty list" (*lista suja*), whose numbers are processed on SmartLab, a platform of the Brazilian labour ministry and the Brazilian section of the International Labour Organization (ILO). The creation of a "dirty list" is one of the measures introduced by the Brazilian government in 2003. The list holds the data of the companies that have been convicted for using *trabalho escravo*, makes them available to the public, and serves as a basis for other enterprises in excluding those who are on this list as business partners or subcontractors. Many banks also deny them eligibility for credit. Enterprises on the list are likewise not allowed to receive public support and subsidized loans.[3] Furthermore, the Pastoral Land Commission (*Comissão Pastoral da Terra*/CPT), one of the most important NGOs fighting this labour condition, maintains a list that contains the names of freed labourers along with some additional information (for example, the gender of the labourers) and includes labour actions from 1995 until 2022. This list, which I was given access to, is one of my other sources. It is important to remember that these statistics only include information on businesses where labourers have been freed from *trabalho escravo*. This means that a lot of information is lacking. Take, for example, the information on sectors: For many years, cattle breed-

3 Vaiddehi Bansal, Jessica Wallach, Juliana Lira Brandão, Sarah Lord, Ninar Taha, Tulay Akoglu, Ligia Kiss and Cathy Zimmerman, "An Intervention-Focused Review of Modern Slave Labor in Brazil's Mining Sector," *World Development* 171, no. 70 (2023); Lisa Carstensen, "Flexibilisierung und Prekarisierung von Arbeit in globalen Produktionsketten – informelle Heimarbeit in der Bekleidungsindustrie in Puebla und São Paulo," Sozial.Geschichte Online 13 (2014): 7–40, http://duepublico.uni-duisburg-essen.de/servlets/DocumentServlet?id=34889 [accessed 05.08.2024]. The *lista suja* can be downloaded here: Ministèrio de Trabalho e Emprego, "Combate ao Trabalho em Condições Análogas às de Escravo," https://www.gov.br/trabalho-e-emprego/pt-br/assuntos/inspecao-do-trabalho/areas-de-atuacao/combate-ao-trabalho-escravo-e-analogo-ao-de-escravo [accessed 16.03.2024].

ing was one of the main sectors in Brazil as a whole, as well as in Pará specifically, where labourers were freed from. But in recent years, the labour inspectorate has started looking more into other sectors. Consequently, sugar cane extraction became the sector where the most labourers were freed from in Brazil in 2022. In Pará, however, cattle breeding stayed on top; interestingly, with retail trade at second place.[4] As retail trade is a relatively new sector for labour inspections looking into *trabalho escravo*, we cannot say for sure that there was little to no *trabalho escravo* in this sector before. Regarding the research, this also means that some questions can only be approached through the filter of the labour inspectorate.

In this article, apart from the internal factors of *trabalho escravo*, external circumstances are also considered as a formative part of this labour condition. This is why it does not only look at the organisation of labour itself, but also at changes in government, power dynamics in the Amazon region, land conflicts, as well as global power dynamics to a certain degree. Regarding the latter, we could observe, for example, that a large part of the unfree labour force in Pará is being used for products sold on the world market, such as beef, vegetable oils, iron ore, precious woods, and biofuels.

When dealing with an international or theoretical context, this article will use the term *unfree labour*, as defined by Tom Brass. In this definition, unfree labour is not a deviation from capitalism but rather emerges from it. It is based on the concept of deproletarianization, which is in turn derived from Karl Marx's concept of proletarianization. While proletarianization entails the expropriation of people's means of production (for example, the land) and, as a matter of survival, the labourers are compelled to sell their labour power, which then becomes a commodity, deproletarianization means that the workers' labour power is also expropriated. It does no longer belong to them, and the labourers are not able to sell it freely anymore. In practice, the last moment at which this

4 SmartLab, "Observatório da Erradicação do Trabalho Escravo e do Tráfico de Pessoas."

becomes obvious is when labourers want to leave their labour condition and are hindered from doing so.[5]

When talking about Brazil, I will use the term *trabalho escravo*. Even though the legal term is *condições análogas ao de escravo,* the more commonly used term is *trabalho escravo*. Since 2003, it has been legally defined as a labour condition in which labourers are either restricted in their freedom of movement, for example, through debt bondage, or are exposed to unreasonably exhausting workdays (*jornadas exaustivas*) or degrading conditions (*condições degradantes*). Only one of the factors has to be present for the labour condition to be defined as *trabalho escravo*.[6] As the terms "exhausting workdays" and "degrading conditions" are not sufficiently self-explanatory, following the legal praxis, it seems they are interpreted as follows: (1) A workday is "exhausting" when a workload which does not permit the reproduction of the labourers' labour power is extorted from them, and (2) conditions are "degrading" when either the living or working conditions under the responsibility of the employer are such that the labourers' health and life are endangered, either intentionally or by omission. In both cases, the law normally only applies when the labourers' lives are in danger.[7] Therefore, apart from holding the labourers by force at the work site, *trabalho escravo* is about the fact that the labourers' lives are not important to the employer and that the extent of their physical power is fully exploited.[8]

The legal definition of *trabalho escravo* is relatively new; the term was already being used by organisations fighting against unfree labour in the 1970s. The introduction of the law against *trabalho escravo* in 1995 was actually the result of the many years of struggle that those organisations fought with the case of José Pereira.

5 Tom Brass, *Labor Regime Change in the Twenty-First Century: Unfreedom, Capitalism and Primitive Accumulation* (Chicago: Haymarket, 2013): 58, 61, 71, 112–13.

6 Lisa Carstensen, "Trabalho Forçado e Tráfico de Pessoas: Uma Análise do Discurso em Instituições e Organizações Internacionais e Brasileiras," *Brasiliana. Journal of Brazilian Studies* 2, no. 2 (2013): 3–31, at 10.

7 Julia Harnoncourt, "Trabalho escravo? Ein historischer Vergleich auf globaler Ebene," *JahrBuch für Forschungen zur Geschichte der Arbeiterbewegung* 14, no. 3 (2015): 63–77, at 63.

8 Organização Internacional do Trabalho, *Perfil dos principais atores envolvidos no trabalho escravo rural no Brasil* (Brasilia: OIT, 2011).

José Pereira, who was a farmhand entrapped in unfree labour, fled in 1989 and tried to report the case afterwards. As no convictions were made, a group of social organisations reported the Brazilian state to the Organization of American States (OAS) in 1994. In the end, the OAS held Brazil responsible, which led to the introduction of the law.[9]

In 1995, *trabalho escravo* was still only defined as a circumstance that made it impossible for the labourer to leave the labour condition, which coincides with the practical part of the definition of unfree labour. Today's definition therefore goes beyond the one of unfree labour and is a result of the praxis of fighting *trabalho escravo*. Admittedly, the changes in the legal definition as well as its interpretation in legal praxis have presented difficulties in terms of statistics, for example, but also with respect to the use of the term in general. Furthermore, even though *trabalho escravo* is the most used term in Brazil, it is not the only one in use. This is why my interview partners frequently employed different terms. In order to not falsify their statements and to ensure transparency, when *trabalho escravo* is being referred to, such terms in the quoted statements are left in Portuguese, with the English translation in brackets.

In Portuguese, a vast array of studies about *trabalho escravo* exists; some are even written in English,[10] French,[11] or in German.[12] In my opinion *Pisando fora da própria sombra* (2004)[13] by Ricardo Rezende Figueira is still one of the most important works concerning this subject. It is a sensitively written anthropological study that deals with *trabalho escravo* in cattle breeding, with the labourers involved in that labour condition, as well as with their home communities, which are Barras (Piauí) and

---

9 Julia Harnoncourt and Miguel Paredes, "Theorizing Human Trafficking and Unfree Labor," *Journal of Global South Studies* 40, no. 1 (2023): 173–212.

10 For example: Lisa Carstensen and Shioban McGrath, "The National Pact to Eradicate Slave Labour in Brazil: A Useful Tool for Unions?" *The National Labour Column* 117 (2012); José de Souza Martins, "The Reappearance of Slavery and the Reproduction of Capital on the Brazilian Frontier," in *Free and Unfree Labour: The Debate Continues*, ed. Tom Brass and Marcel van der Linden (Bern: Lang, 1997): 281–302.

11 For example: Ricardo Rezende Figueira, Adonia A. Prado and Rafael F. Palmeira, "L'esclavage contemporain et ses transformations en Amazonie brésilienne: Les témoignages des victimes," *Brésil(s)* 11 (2017).

12 Carstensen, "Flexibilisierung und Prekarisierung von Arbeit."

13 Rezende Figueira, *Pisando fora da própria sombra*.

communities in the northeast of Mato Grosso. These labourers leave these communities to mostly work in the South of Pará. In the study, he is especially concerned with the perspective of the labourers and their basic social conditions before and after entering this labour relation. In his book, Rezende Figueira offers a deep insight into the living conditions and trajectories of these labourers. He was able to achieve this through interviews with the labourers and their families, whom he had access to due to his position as a priest and long-time employee of the CPT.

Another important and newer work is the compilation by Leonardo Sakamoto and Renato Bignami titled *Escravidão contemporânea* (2020), which, in different sections, gives an overview of the topic through, for example, the profiles of the labourers or the laws against *trabalho escravo* in Brazil.[14] Other interesting examples are the collection of articles edited by Rezende Figueira, Antunes Prado, and Galvão (2017),[15] and the volume published by the Faculty of Law of the Federal University of Minas Gerais (2018),[16] both of which, like a lot of the Brazilian literature on the topic, are focussed on the legal implications. Other authors are more interested in examining concepts and use *trabalho escravo* in Brazil as case studies. One example is Martig's article on "Slaving Zones, Contemporary Slavery and Citizenship" (2018),[17] where he tries to apply the concept of "slaving zones", which differentiates between zones where "slave labour" is needed and ones where the workforce is taken from. Another is Carstensen's article on "Unfree Labour, Migration and Racism",[18] where she attempts to show the interlinkages between racism and unfree labour based on *trabalho escravo* in Brazil.

14 Leonardo Sakamoto and Renato Bignami, *Escravidão contemporânea* (São Paulo: Editora Contexto, 2020).

15 Ricardo Rezende Figueira, Adonia Antunes Prado and Edna M. Galvão, eds., *Trabalho Escravo Contemporâneo: Estudos sobre ações e atores* (Rio de Janeiro: Mauad X, 2017).

16 Lívia Mendes Moreira Miraglia, Julianna do Nascimento Hernandez and Rayhanna Fernandes de Souza Oliveira, eds. *Trabalho Escravo Contemporâneo: Conceituação, desafios e perspectivas* (Rio de Janeiro: Lumen Juris, 2018).

17 Alexis Martig, "Slaving Zones, Contemporary Slavery and Citizenship: Reflections from the Brazilian Case," in *Slaving Zones: Cultural Identities, Ideologies, and Institutions in the Evolution of Global Slavery*, ed. Jeff Fynn-Paul and Damian A. Pargas (Leiden: Brill, 2018): 336–59.

18 Lisa Carstensen, "Unfree Labour, Migration and Racism: Towards an Analytical Framework," *Global Labour Journal* 12, no. 1 (2021).

Furthermore, the CPT publishes a report on conflicts in the countryside every year, which always contains an article about new developments regarding *trabalho escravo*.[19]

Much less is written on *trabalho escravo* in Pará. There is, for example, an interesting study on this labour condition in Pará's wood-cutting sector, which was commissioned by the CPT.[20] There is also a dissertation on a specific case of *trabalho escravo* on the *fazenda* (estate or large farm) Cabaceiras – incidentally the same fazenda, where the labourer I interviewed worked on.[21] Also in her book, Carstensen compares *trabalho escravo* in the textile industry in Sao Paulo with that found in charcoal production for the steel industry in Carajás (Pará).[22] And then there is my book on *trabalho escravo* in Pará's agricultural sector, which also briefly discusses the situation after the coup against Dilma Rousseff in 2016.[23] The changes in the administration of *trabalho escravo* during the presidency of Michel Temer (2016–2018) and Jair Bolsonaro (2019–2022) have barely been explored. Articles or works dedicated to the topic during those periods are practically non-existent, and the present article intends to change this, while putting a focus on Pará.

In order to understand the issue, the present article will first describe the legal definition as well as the typical trajectory of the labourers under these labour conditions in Pará's agricultural sector. Then, the classical structure of a *fazenda,* a large estate or farm in the Amazon region, will be explained to further present the historical development of the law and the main mechanisms established to combat *trabalho escravo.* At this point, but also in the following sections, the article will be dealing with

19 See, for example, the last one: Carolina Motoki, Brígida Rocha dos Santos and Waldeci Campos de Souza, "De 1995 a 2022: o trabalho escravo contemporâneo a partir dos dados sistematizados pela Comissão Pastoral da Terra," in "Conflitos no Campo: Brasil 2022," Goiânia, 2023: 141–61.

20 CDVDH/CB, and CPT, *Por debaixo da Floresta: Amazonia paraense saqueada com trabalho escravo* (São Paulo: Urutu-Branco, 2017).

21 Carlos J. Barros, "O sonho se faz a mão e sem permissão: 'Escravidão temporânea' e reforma agraria no sudeste do Pará" (PhD diss., Universidade de São Paulo, 2011).

22 Anne Lisa Carstensen, *Das Dispositiv moderne Sklavenarbeit: Umkämpfte Arbeitsverhältnisse in Brasilien*, International Labour Studies 23 (Frankfurt: Campus Verlag, 2019).

23 Julia Harnoncourt, *Unfreie Arbeit: Trabalho escravo in der brasilianischen Landwirtschaft*, Edition Kritische Forschung (Wien: Promedia, 2018).

the changes that occurred due to the political turn in Brazil with the coup against Dilma Rousseff in 2016, and then it will go deeper into the factors influencing *trabalho escravo*. The violent treatment of the labourers is anchored in historical developments, for example, in the gendered images and racialization of the labourers, as well as in the imagined need for a continued colonization of the Amazon region, which is linked to land grabbing and land concentration. Under former President Jair Bolsonaro, conservative gender images were upheld, racist views were expressed more overtly, and environmental protection for the Amazon region was continuously diminished, as was the protection for the land of Indigenous people; thus, we can assume a strong (negative) impact on the fight against *trabalho escravo*. Furthermore, as this labour relation is also anchored in the global capitalist market, the article will take a brief look at this interconnection and into the possibility of gaining novel perspectives with the new government of Luiz Lula Inácio da Silva.

The Vicious Cycle of *trabalho escravo*

Walk Free, an international human rights group, estimates that around one million people in Brazil are trapped in "modern slavery".[24] This number is problematic as the term follows a different definition (that of modern slavery, not of *trabalho escravo*), but it might still serve as a very rough estimate. In terms of the number of labourers freed from *trabalho escravo*, between 1995 and 2023, around 61,700 were found to be working in conditions of *trabalho escravo* in Brazil as a whole, and around 13,400 of them were freed in Pará. In 2023 alone, there were around 1,400 labourers freed from these conditions (versus an annual average of 2,000) in the country, while the total amount of those freed from *trabalho escravo* in Pará was 12, much lower than the annual average of 460 labourers.[25] Comparing the first numbers to the latter ones, we can assume in any case that there are a lot of labourers doing *trabalho*

---

24 Walk Free, "The Global Slavery Index 2023," https://www.walkfree.org/global-slavery-index/downloads/ [accessed 26.08.2023].

25 There is a difference in the number of labourers found in and freed from *trabalho*

escravo who are never freed by the state. The dark figure is therefore certainly considerable. One of those cases is Andreas[26], the agricultural labourer I interviewed during my research visit to Pará in 2014. He had worked in *trabalho escravo* years before our interview. As he just left this labour condition, before the intervention of the labour inspectorate and without reporting his labour condition, he is one of the cases who will never appear in the statistics.

Generally, *trabalho escravo* in Pará's agricultural sector is described as a cycle.[27] Rural labourers who live in poverty are persuaded by labour recruiters, called *gatos*, with false promises to enter into a labour relation and to travel with them to the work site. The fraudulent debts are incurred as soon as the journey begins, since the labourers are charged with everything. Once at the workplace, the labourers are forced to live and work at the same site. Everything they need to survive and get the job done, such as food or tools, is deducted from their wages at inflated prices. In addition, they have to live and work under terrible conditions. The main issues here are the quality of the food, the drinking water, and the housing, as well as long hours and strenuous work. In addition to the debt, the labourers are often prevented from leaving the workplace by armed guards and the lack of infrastructure. And when the labourers, who are usually no longer needed after a few months, are dismissed and abandoned at an unknown location, they are forced to exit their labour relation without any money due to their debt and the generally low wages. They therefore find themselves in the same situation as before or even worse, and the vicious cycle begins anew. Which is why some labourers are freed more than once from *trabalho escravo*.

The following sub-sections will describe the individual stages of *trabalho escravo* in more detail.

---

escravo, as some have either fled or died, see for example: SmartLab, "Observatório da Erradicação do Trabalho Escravo e do Tráfico de Pessoas."

26 Names of people who are not known to the general public are anonymized. Full names are not anonymized.

27 See, for example, the learning materials of the educational program Fascículos: "Ciclo do Trabalho Escravo Contemporâneo," https://escravonempensar.org.br/biblioteca/ciclo-do-trabalho-escravo-contemporaneo-2/ [accessed 07.04.2024].

Initial Situation of the Labourers

Poverty and money problems are the most common reason for labourers to accept any kind of work, since there is hardly any other way of surviving.[28] This does not necessarily mean that they end up in *trabalho escravo*. But the usual working conditions in the countryside of Pará are very hard, and labour is poorly paid. Free and unfree labourers often work side by side, with small differences in hierarchy, pay, and length of service. Even the free labourers on the *fazendas* only manage to cover their survival expenses with their wages. Poor nutrition and inadequate housing, for example, are seen as normal by the labourers since they are used to it from their general living conditions and other jobs.[29] Luana, an activist of the Pastoral Land Commission (*Comissão Pastoral da Terra/* CPT) in Tucumã, said in an interview in 2014:

> Normally, when he [the labourer] becomes an employee, he has all the rights of all employees regardless of the life he has outside [the work…]. The labourer himself thinks he doesn't need it [his labour rights] and even thinks it's normal.[30]

Most of the labourers originate from the neighbour states of Pará. They know the risks of looking for a job in the region, and as Pará generally has higher wages, at least for the labourers coming from Maranhão,[31] the risk must be taken as there is hardly any alternative.[32] Apart from the hopeless financial situation, other labourers report, among other

---

28 Ricardo Rezende Figueira, "A Persistência da Escravidão Ilegal no Brasil," in *Desafios aos Direitos Humanos no Brasil Contemporâneo*, ed. Brion Maybury-Lewis and Sonia Ranincheski (Brasília: Verbena, 2011): 49–64, at 58–59.

29 Iana/CPT, Interview by Julia Harnoncourt, 22.10.2014, Xinguara.

30 Luana/CPT, Interview by Julia Harnoncourt, 20.11.2014, Tucumã. All the interviews have originally been conducted in Portuguese and are translated by the author.

31 As Maranhão has the lowest average income in Brazil (FGV, "R$ – Renda Média da População – UF," https://cps.fgv.br/r-renda-media-da-populacao-uf-2020 [accessed 03.03.2024]).

32 Shioban McGrath and Kendra Strauss, "Unfreedom and Workers' Power: Ever-Present Possibilities," in *Handbook of the International Political Economy of Production*, ed. Kees van der Pijl (Cheltenham: Edward Elgar, 2015): 299–317.

things, the loss of work, problems in the family or with others in the hometown, as well as their own wishes, dreams, and hopes, the idea of a better life, and the desire to get to know something new as their motivation for going to Pará to try their luck.[33]

Another point that increases the precariousness of the situation of the labourers is their non-existence in the eyes of the state bureaucracy, especially the labourers from peripheral areas, as they do not appear in any register and have no birth certificate or any other document confirming their existence and identity. As a result, it is not possible for these labourers, in practice, to access their theoretical civil rights.[34] Jônatas Andrade, a labour judge who received an award for defending human rights in 2012,[35] affirmed this connection in 2014:

> Anyone who submits to anything – *escravidão* (slavery), exploitation, exploitation of their dignity – does not enjoy basic citizenship rights. They don't have a home, they don't have a roof, they don't have labour rights. [...] The *trabalhador escravo* in general doesn't even exist, because he doesn't have a birth certificate. [...] These people, from a legal point of view, don't even exist. [...] So, it's not for nothing that these people are enticed [to leave] these pockets of misery in the hinterland of the Northeast, where there is no education, where there is no health system. It is there that the *gatos*, who are the intermediaries, go to get the labourers to be *escravizados* (enslaved).[36]

In some cases, like in that of Andreas, the labourer I interviewed, the person who gets the labourers the job is a relative or a friend. However, mostly, it is a professional labour enticer (*gato*), whose job is to get desperate labourers to agree to come with them.

---

33 Padre Paulinho/CPT, Interview by Julia Harnoncourt, 11.11.2014, Belém; Patricía T. Maranhão Costa, "Fighting Forced Labour: The Example of Brazil," Special Action Programme to Combat Forced Labour, Geneva, 2009: 70.

34 Rezende Figueira. *Pisando fora da própria sombra*: 143, 281.

35 Dudu Zé "Marabá: juiz Jônatas Andrade irá receber Prêmio Direitos Humanos 2012 das mãos da presidente Dilma," 06.12.2012, http://www.zedudu.com.br/?p=26837 [accessed 27.08.2023].

36 Jônatas Andrade, Interview by Julia Harnoncourt, 30.10.2014, Marabá.

Journey to the Workplace

The journey to the *fazenda* is very prominent in the literature and in sources about *trabalho escravo*. In the descriptions of the vicious cycle of this labour relation, the journey from the labourer's home region to the work site is usually classified into two or three types: (1) the labourer is recruited in the home region and travels under the supervision of the *gato*, (2) the labourer travels on his own and is then recruited, and (3) the labourer becomes a migrant labourer (*peão de trecho*); he no longer has a home.[37]

The journey under the control of the *gato* is the most mentioned type in the sources since mechanisms of coercion are already built into it. The debt system also begins at the time of recruitment. The *gatos* promise formal work with good housing and food, for which the labourers would not have to pay. In addition, they usually leave money for the families of the labourers. Their need is therefore alleviated in the short term. This advance of money is an important reason for the labourers to go with the *gatos*.[38] In our 2014 interview, labour judge Jônatas Andrade summarised the thoughts of the labourers as follows: "He [the *gato*] gives me a bottle of cachaça. He leaves 200 reais for my family. Is there anything better?"[39]

The trip itself also generates debt despite the *gatos'* promise of it being for free. Methods such as withholding official documents would already be in use at this point.[40] The labourers are taken to an area they are unfamiliar with, far from any infrastructure and without any means of transport, which also deprives the labourers of their freedom as it is practically impossible to leave from such places autonomously. One labourer described this situation to the state organs when he and eighteen other labourers were freed from *trabalho escravo* at the cattle breeding *fazenda* Bela Vista in Altamira (Pará). He testified "[...] that he

37 Maranhão Costa, "Fighting Forced Labour": 70–72; Rezende Figueira, *Pisando fora da própria sombra*: 117.

38 Raimundo Nonato do Nascimento Pereira and Francisco Almeida Rodriguez, "Formulário de denúncia de trabalho escravo," 20.06.2008, CPT Xinguara.

39 Andrade, Interview 2014.

40 McGrath and Strauss, "Unfreedom and Workers' Power: Ever-Present Possibilities."

didn't leave because he was trapped there since there was no road and he could only return by plane; that he thinks that everyone also felt trapped in the same way he did [...]".[41]

Another function of the trip is to rip labourers out of their social networks, thereby weakening their position.[42] Luana, the activist from the CPT in Tucumã, also described this in 2014:

> They are not able to exploit people from here, from the region, in the same way that they can exploit a person from there. Because those people don't have friends here, they don't know where the union is, they don't know anyone. [...] If you take someone from Tucumã, within a couple of days he will have help, he can get out easily, he can run away, he manages. [...] So, this issue of taking the person out of their place, their comfort zone, is already a way of caging the person. The person is left there with no way out. Because when the night comes, he is in the middle of the woods. He doesn't even know which side the city is on.[43]

Since the Brazilian Federal Highway Police has also been vigilant for labourers being transported for some years now,[44] one can assume that this phenomenon might have decreased, even though there are no figures available on the forms of transportation.

Labourers who travel to Pará alone stay in accommodations called "hotels". To ensure that the labourers pay their bills, the "hotel" owners withhold their luggage and official documents. *Gatos* also go to such "hotels" in search of labourers. They offer to settle the labourers' debts, after which the labourers would then be in debt to them or the *fazen-*

41 Fiscalía, "Resumo da ação fiscal," 2008, Archive CPT Xinguara. English translation from the original in Portuguese by the author.
42 Maranhão Costa, "Fighting Forced Labour": 15, 62.
43 Luana/CPT, Interview 2014.
44 Governamento Brasil, "PRF em Operação Conjunta com o Ministério Público do Trabalho atua no Combate ao Trabalho Escravo," https://www.gov.br/prf/pt-br/noticias/estaduais/goias/2022/novembro/prf-em-operacao-conjunta-com-o-ministerio-publico-do-trabalho-atua-no-combate-ao-trabalho-escravo [accessed 23.02.2024].

deiros[45] (the owner of the *fazenda*). The "hotel" owners therefore also take part in the recruitment process for *trabalho escravo*.[46]

In 2014, Iana, a long-standing CPT activist from Xinguara, described the *peões de trecho* as "[...]people who have generally lost family ties. [...] So, coming also from the countryside, and being away from their family, having lost contact with them, they go from *fazenda* to *fazenda*".[47]

Conditions on the *fazenda*

Andreas, the labourer I managed to interview, was hired as a machine operator at a *fazenda* called Cabaceiras. The position is somewhat better than that of many other labourers as some training is needed to use the machines. Most of the labourers doing *trabalho escravo* are hired to clear the area. Despite his position, Andreas still had to starve there, and his wages were always paid far too late. He claimed that after he was hired ...

> Time went by, two months, five months, six months, a year, and the *fazenda* began to delay paying its staff. [...] All of them, cowboys, foremen and heavy machine operators, which was my area, [...] and the people who did manual labour. And then we went up to two months without receiving payment, [...] and it got to the point where people ate only mangoes and flour.

> Julia: And how was it? Did you have to pay for the food yourself? Andreas: That was on us. But for us to buy, we had to receive our salary from the *fazenda*, right? And we asked the manager of the *fazenda*, and he claimed that the *fazendeiro* had not given the payment for the employees.[48]

45 As most of the *fazendeiros* are men, the masculine form is used here.
46 Maranhão Costa, "Fighting Forced Labour": 58–59, 70–71.
47 Iana/CPT, Interview 2014.
48 Andreas and Maria/MST, Interview by Julia Harnoncourt, 01.11.2014, Acampamento Hugo Chavez, Pará.

There is normally a shop on the *fazenda*, which is the only place where the labourers could buy food, products for personal hygiene, tools, protective clothing, and so on. Everything is sold to them at horrendous prices. This is an important part of the mechanism that promotes the accumulation of debt. The accumulated debts would often be so high that the labourers would no longer receive their wages and end up only working off their debts. The hope of the labourers to get some money at some point is maintained for as long as possible in order to guarantee the highest possible work input. It is common for labourers doing *trabalho escravo* to have no control over their debts. It is the company alone that has an overview of the amount they owe. In most cases, the labourers only find out over time that they are in debt. Despite the obvious illegitimacy of the debt, the labourers feel obliged to pay it.

Food problems are one of the biggest complaints raised by the labourers.[49] They, as well as governmental and non-governmental organisations dealing with this issue, find this situation particularly cruel and absurd since most of the companies raise cattle, that is, they produce meat for sale, while the labourers are starving. Not only the lack of food is repeatedly mentioned, but also its poor quality. Labourers frequently bear witness to mouldy meat and worms.[50] Food and food distribution are often used to discipline the labourers.[51] On some *fazendas*, labourers are denied food as punishment for bad behaviour.[52] Andreas also mentioned the arbitrary distribution of meat that had in part already gone bad, but which the labourers were still forced to buy.[53] Starving even while working seems to have been especially traumatic for Andreas, as he kept coming back to this issue in his interview:

---

49 McGrath, Strauss, “Unfreedom and Workers’ Power: Ever-Present Possibilities.”

50 Organização Internacional do Trabalho, *Perfil dos principais atores envolvidos no trabalho escravo rural no Brasil*: 48.

51 McGrath, Strauss, “Unfreedom and Workers’ Power: Ever-Present Possibilities.”

52 Neide Estreci, *Escravos da desigualdade: Um estudo dobre o uso repressivo da força de trabalho hoje* (Rio de Janeiro: Centro Edelstein de Pesquisas Sociais, 2008): 44.

53 Andreas and Maria/MST Interview 2014.

> Have we been hungry? Yes, we have. At one time we had to split up. Some were doing something there. Others went fishing in the area. [...] So we could survive. And I went hunting with a colleague of mine, and we even killed a jaguar and fed on it. [...] While having employment, while working, right?[54]

Other labourers who have worked on the Cabaceiras also specifically remember the situations in which they had to go hungry.[55]

Apart from the food, the supply of drinking water is another source of constant complaints.[56] Generally, labourers have related how they would have to drink from the same water source as the animals, and how some would get sick from the water.[57] At the *fazenda* Cabaceiras, it was similar; there was hardly any water, and what was available caused the labourers stomach problems.[58] But not only the water caused illnesses; a lot of labourers suffered from malaria or yellow fewer, for example. And because of the terrible working conditions, accidents are also common under *trabalho escravo.* Other illnesses are caused by the labour activity, for example, by spraying pesticides and herbicides without any protective gear.[59] When the labourers get sick, it is usual the labourers doing

54 Ibid.

55 Leonardo Sakamoto, "Perfil de uma família escravocrata," *Observatorio Social* 2004, no. 6: 28–32, at 30.

56 McGrath, Strauss, "Unfreedom and Workers' Power: Ever-Present Possibilities."

57 Leandro da Silva Farias, "Formulário de denúncia de trabalho escravo," 12.09.2012, CPT Xinguara; do Nascimento Pereira, Almeida Rodriguez, "Formulário de denúncia de trabalho escravo."

58 Andreas and Maria/MST, Interview 2014; Carlos Juliano Barros, "Conquista da Fazenda Cabaceiras: Escravidão temporária, luta de classes e reforma agráriano sul do Pará," *Anais Encontro Nacional dos Geógrafos* 16 (2010).

59 Brazil is actually one of the countries with the highest use of pesticides, together with the United States and China. Vinicius Konchinski, "Brasil usa mais agrotóxicos que Estados Unidos e China juntos," *Brasil de Fato*, 05.02.2024, https://www.brasildefato.com.br/2024/02/05/brasil-usa-mais-agrotoxicos-que-estados-unidos-e-china-juntos [accessed 04.04.2024]. For the general use of pesticides and their effect on the health of the labourers, see, for example: Mariana Portela de-Assis, Raquel Cristine Barcella, Janaína Chiogna Padilha, Hildegard Hedwig Pohl and Suzane Beatriz Frantz Krug, "Health Problems in Agricultural Workers Occupationally Exposed to Pesticides," *Revista brasileira de medicina do trabalho publicação oficial da Associacao Nacional de Medicina do Trabalho-ANAMT* 18, no. 3 (2021): 352–63.

trabalho escravo find no assistance from their employers or their representatives.[60] Andreas also talked about a colleague who got poisoned by the products he had sprayed:

> Julia: Did the issue of protection from working with poison exist? Andreas: No, it didn't. The only thing in existence was a little cloth that nobody even used. [...] The thing the manager said was to use milk, to drink plenty of milk. There was no lack of milk for the people who sprayed poison, but no protection, no adequate clothing, not even a mask. I knew a guy who got sick from the poison. He got intoxicated. [...] He lost weight. He had a breathing problem and was vomiting every hour. [...] He spent about three months on the farm still working [while intoxicated]. Then his condition got worse. They took him to the hospital. We never saw him again. [...] He left the farm. He asked to be paid. I was even one of those who advised him not to settle the accounts; the farm had to take care of his treatment. He said: 'No. [...] I'm going home to my relatives, to stay close to my family, they will take care of me.' [...] After he left, I lost contact [with him]. I don't know if he's alive, I don't know if he died, or if he was cured. And there were other cases, but I didn't know these labourers.[61]

The pesticides do not only intoxicate the labourers directly working with them; in some cases, they also seep into the drinking water. Consequences are often stomach pains, headaches, and fungal-like illnesses.[62] When they get sick, the labourers have to take care of themselves, a fact that was also experienced by Andreas:

> Sometimes it was the employees themselves who went to the road and searched for a car. At the time, there was a lot of malaria. [...] I also caught malaria twice there. And then we would run out for transport.

60 Ângela Maria de Castro Gomes, "Repression and Changes in Slave-Like Labor in Brazil: In the Present Time and Uses of the Past," *Revista Brasileira de História* 32, no. 64 (2012): 151–67, at 156.

61 Andreas and Maria/MST, Interview 2014.

62 Antonio Brexior Pereira and Jarbas Henrique Sampaio Azevedo, "Formulário de denúncia de trabalho escravo," 19.10.2009, CPT Xinguara.

> We would bring them [the sick labourers] to the shacks – the shacks made of plastic sheets – we would take the employees, put them in a vehicle, and take them to the hospital. And the *fazendeiro* did not give any assistance in this area. We had to find ways to take care of ourselves.[63]

Neglect of the lives of the labourers as well as of their labour and human rights is an important aspect of *trabalho escravo.*[64]

Despite knowing about the poor working conditions in agriculture, a large proportion of the labourers still feels disappointed and shocked when they arrive at their workplace. Their desperation intensifies over time. Their debts continue to mount, and there is no prospect of earning any money. At the same time, they realize that their lives and survival are of very little to no importance to those in charge: they lack medical care, the necessary protective equipment, as well as food and hydration appropriate for such labour. Also, shacks made out of black plastic sheets (*lona preta*), which serve as the labourers' home on the *fazenda,* are a recurring motif.[65] These shacks do not protect them against the rain or the sun, they do not allow for ventilation, and they are often overcrowded. Frequently, the shacks have to be built by the labourers themselves. Further grievances include the lack of sanitary facilities.[66] A particularly important factor in *trabalho escravo* is the low wages, which do not measure up to what was promised, and the already-mentioned debt system, which is very common. The remuneration of the labourers is often calculated dissimilarly (for example, fixed salary, payment per hour, or according to performance), which leads to a hierarchization between the labourers and to their different life and work realities, thus disrupting solidarity among them.

Violence, or the threat of it, is also an important part of the regime. There have been many cases of labourers being killed. Several secret

63 Andreas and Maria/MST, Interview 2014.

64 Luana/CPT, Interview 2014.

65 Barros, "Conquista da Fazenda Cabaceiras"; de Castro Gomes. "Repression and Changes in Slave-Like Labor in Brazil"; Iana/CPT, Interview 2014; Maranhão Costa, "Fighting Forced Labour": 61.

66 De Castro Gomes, "Repression and Changes in Slave-Like Labor in Brazil": 156.

cemeteries have been found on some *fazendas*,[67] including the Cabaceiras, where Andreas worked.[68] Torture is also sometimes part of the regime. (The regime can therefore range from the omission of basic rights to active torture and killings.) Physical violence is used when labourers flee or demand to be paid. But in many cases, there is also a constant threat of violence from the armed guards who are watching the labourers while they are working. With regard to the legal determination of *trabalho escravo*, these armed guards (*pistoleiros*) are an important element as they provide evidence for the lack of freedom of movement.[69] Punishments for resistance and alleged misconduct are also often spoken of. Locking or tying up labourers, as well as refusing to give them food, inflicting burns, and subjecting them to beatings seem to be common methods. Verbal abuse, threats, and personal attacks are also common, and labourers perceive them as humiliation. This leads to constant anxiety and stress. This treatment, together with the living conditions on the *fazenda*, is dehumanizing for many labourers. Labourers often describe their conditions as being treated "like animals".[70]

A Classical *fazenda*

There are different roles and hierarchies in the system of *trabalho escravo*. The *fazendeiro*, the manager, the *gato*, and the armed guards have already been mentioned, as well as the labourers and their different categorizations through distinct tasks, employment forms, and calculations of their salary. The unequal treatment of the labourers and the use of hierarchies have a disciplining effect.[71] Which functions exist on the

67 Binka Le Breton, *Vidas roubadas: A escravidão moderna na Amazônia Brasileira* (São Paulo: Loyola, 2002): 80.

68 Cida de Oliveira, "MST foi decisivo em desapropriação de terras com trabalho escravo, diz pesquisa," Rede Brasil Atual, 12.03.2012, http://www.redebrasilatual.com.br/cidadania/2012/03/mst-foi-decisivo-em-desapropriacao-de-fazenda-com-trabalho-escravo-aponta-estudo-da-usp [accessed 28.08.2023].

69 Maranhão Costa, "Fighting Forced Labour": 56.

70 Carstensen, "Trabalho Forçado e Tráfico de Pessoas": 7; de Castro Gomes, "Repression and Changes in Slave-Like Labor in Brazil."

71 Estreci, *Escravos da desigualdade*: 98–99.

individual *fazendas* and whether the *fazendeiros* and their families live on site depend on the size of the company and the type of activity. Most of the *fazendas* in Pará that use *trabalho escravo* raise cattle, but enterprises that breed other animals or grow agricultural products such as soybeans or sugar cane also use this form of exploitation.

Just to name one example: The owners of the *fazenda* Cabaceiras, where Andreas worked, were three brothers, with Evandro Mutran being the one directly responsible for it. Their cattle are internationally known as they are one of the most important Nelore cattle breeders in Brazil.[72] Evandro Mutran owned three *fazendas* in Pará – the Cabaceiras, the Peruano, and the Baguá – and others in different parts of Brazil. Andreas mentioned that he also worked on the Peruano for six months. The labourers often have to work on another *fazenda* for a short time if this is demanded of them. Even though all three *fazendas* were a bit different, cases of *trabalho escravo* have been found on all of them.[73] "Each one [*fazenda*] had a different manager and on each one, the environment and the relationship of the employees with the managers were different. Even on the Peruano, the most beautiful, most preserved farm, [...] *trabalho escravo* was found", Andreas recounted.[74] As in many cases, these *fazendeiros* do not live on their fazendas; Evandro Mutran lived in Belém, the capital of Pará.

The Mutran family made a fortune selling Brazil nuts in the 1920s and also became politically influential in the Marabá region in the 1950s. Later, the family began to devote themselves to cattle. They are now one of the richest families in Pará, and there are rumours of horrific, violent crimes and murders having been committed by its members.[75] It is typi-

---

72 De Oliveira, "MST foi decisivo em desapropriação de terras com trabalho escravo, diz pesquisa"; "Pecuária perde mais um grande nelorista e 'Rei do gado do Pará'," CompreRural, 01.03.2024, https://www.comprerural.com/pecuaria-perde-mais-um-grande-nelorista-bene-mutran/ [accessed 04.04.2024].

73 Barros, "Conquista da Fazenda Cabaceiras"; Le Breton, *Vidas roubadas*: 79–80; de Oliveira, "MST foi decisivo em desapropriação de terras com trabalho escravo, diz pesquisa."

74 Andreas and Maria/MST, Interview 2014.

75 Barros, "Conquista da Fazenda Cabaceiras"; Le Breton, *Vidas roubadas*: 79–80; de Oliveira, "MST foi decisivo em desapropriação de terras com trabalho escravo, diz pesquisa."

cal for large agricultural companies in Pará to be owned by influential families or individuals. Their power is not only created on the *fazenda*, but also through societal conditions, as Antonho, an employee of the Tucumã Municipality Office for Agricultural Affairs, described in 2014:

> Imagine a rural labourer from Maranhão, Piauí, Tocantins, in a poor situation, meeting a *fazendeiro* who has influence in the Chamber of Deputies, who is connected to the mayor, who is connected to a big businessman in the region, who has social notoriety and is well regarded, who is there in church. So, he [the labourer] feels powerless in the face of all this.[76]

Like the Mutran brothers, *fazendeiros* often own more than one *fazenda* where *trabalho escravo* exists. Unlike Evandro, many of them come from the southern states of Brazil, which has to do with the fact that those are more prosperous states.[77] The nature of the relationship between large landowners and the labourers depends strongly on the size of the *fazenda* and the personal involvement of the *fazendeiros* in their enterprise. Some *fazendeiros* live on their *fazenda*, others look after things from time to time and pursue other professions. On these *fazendas*, the relationship between the owner and the labourers is impersonal. Personal relationships involving individual paternalism and obligations, as well as feelings of gratitude, protection, and the like, also occur. This is especially true in smaller enterprises where the owner lives on the *fazenda*, and his role is often that of a strict father.[78]

Two basic types of agricultural entrepreneurs are evident. The first type is that of a modern capitalist. They only see numbers and profit. The people who represent or produce these numbers do not matter to them. The second is the paternalistic type. These *fazendeiros* are used to being in charge as their family has enjoyed regional power over a long

76 Antonho/Secretaria Municipal de Agricultura Tucumã, Interview by Julia Harnoncourt, 23.11.2014, Tucumã.

77 For the average income by state in 2020, see: FGV, "R$ – Renda Média da População – UF."

78 Maranhão Costa, "Fighting Forced Labour": 65, 67–68.

period of time. For them, other people are natural subordinates because they do not know any other way. These companies are often described as traditional.[79]

The paternalistic/traditional entrepreneurs expect gratitude from their labourers and society since they assume that they are already helping out by creating jobs. Their labourers are supposedly used to the bad conditions. In addition, the *fazendeiros* argue that they pay taxes and support Brazil's economic development with their company under the adverse circumstances of the Amazon region. Thus, they see themselves as pioneers.[80]

The capitalist type of entrepreneur often uses cutting edge technology such as artificial insemination, clone production, modern veterinary care as well as "direct planting", a planting technique designed to reduce soil damage. The organisation of the company is bureaucratic, and everything is divided into different departments. Usually there is even a research and development department.[81] These entrepreneurs legitimize their behaviour when *trabalho escravo* is identified by claiming that they knew nothing about it. After all, they are hardly present on their properties, and certainly not in conflict situations. Another way for entrepreneurs to avoid responsibility is by outsourcing. Xavier Plassat, CPT Brazil's organiser of actions against *trabalho escravo*, mentioned this strategy in 2014: "The outsourcing mechanism lets them [the *fazendeiros*] do anything on their land without getting involved with how the labourers are treated."[82] In this case, a supposedly independent company is hired to carry out the desired activities on a *fazenda* that uses *trabalho escravo*. However, this service company is often created specifically to work for a single entrepreneur.[83] And although these entrepreneurs live far away, they are still informed about the most important events and,

---

79 Organização Internacional do Trabalho, *Perfil dos principais atores envolvidos no trabalho escravo rural no Brasil*: 132–37.

80 Maranhão Costa, "Fighting Forced Labour": 65.

81 Organização Internacional do Trabalho, *Perfil dos principais atores envolvidos no trabalho escravo rural no Brasil*: 132–37.

82 Xavier Plassat/CPT, Interview by Julia Harnoncourt, 26.11.2014, Araguaína.

83 Organização Internacional do Trabalho, *Perfil dos principais atores envolvidos no trabalho escravo rural no Brasil*: 36.

in most cases, know very well what is happening. Ultimately, the same companies can be reported for *trabalho escravo* on several occasions.[84]

Bigger *fazendas* have a manager who replaces the *fazendeiro* when he is not there, especially when the *fazendeiro* does not live on site. He manages the *fazenda* and organises the work. In the literature, he is very seldomly mentioned.[85] The manager on the Cabaceiras was Genêncio Chimoka.[86] Andreas saw him as a rather positive figure and perceived him as friendly.[87]

The *gatos* follow the manager in the hierarchy. Some *fazendas* have only one *gato*, while bigger ones normally have several, also distinguished according to hierarchies and tasks. Their main task is to hire labourers. Their expertise lies primarily in procuring labourers as quickly and cheaply as possible. In order to accomplish this, they promise them certain labour conditions, which are not kept; this is why the labourers perceive them as dishonest exploiters. In addition to hiring labourers, some of the *gatos* also take on surveillance tasks, which are often done with a lot of violence and threats. Depending on how well known a *gato* is and on the size of the *fazenda*, his power position, habitus, and areas of responsibility would also vary. The "little *gatos*" or *gatinhos* hardly differ in appearance from the labourers. They mostly also work together with them. Some of these *gatinhos* are victims themselves and cannot leave the *fazenda*. They are sometimes even acquaintances, relatives, or friends of the labourers.[88] The "big *gatos*" have their own service companies, which provide labourers to several *fazendas* and rely on a network of accomplices: the "hotel" owners, drivers, policemen who turn a blind eye, etc.[89] Many *fazendeiros* place the blame on the *gatos*, especially

84 Maranhão Costa, "Fighting Forced Labour": 68.

85 For example, in this detailed work describing the different roles on the *fazendas*, there are separate sections for the labourers and the *gatos*, while the manager is rarely mentioned: Organização Internacional do Trabalho, *Perfil dos principais atores envolvidos no trabalho escravo rural no Brasil.*

86 Sakamoto, "Perfil de uma família escravocrata": 30.

87 Andreas and Maria/MST, Interview 2014.

88 Organização Internacional do Trabalho, *Perfil dos principais atores envolvidos no trabalho escravo rural no Brasil*: 17, 88.

89 Maranhão Costa, "Fighting Forced Labour": 68.

when they work as subcontractors.[90] In 1993, a *fazendeiro* allegedly said to a Brazilian newspaper: "My contract is with the *gato*. If he killed his father, mother, or an agricultural labourer, I don't care. What matters is that he gives me the cleaned land."[91]

The armed guards are subordinated to the *gatos* and are tasked to make sure that only authorized people leave and enter the *fazenda*. They also control the quality and speed of the production. Their very presence and their carrying of guns work as an implicit threat. But their duties also include the active use of force.[92] The guards normally come from the same social strata as the labourers, and they include labourers who were promoted because they knew how to handle weapons. They dress similarly and listen to the same music. Former policemen also work in this position.[93]

On very large *fazendas,* which exist to a relatively high degree in Pará – which is third on the list of states in which large estates can be found[94] – there are also well-trained staff working, such as veterinarians, agronomists, and teachers for the children of regular employees. These employees are usually well paid and enjoy regular employment.

The remaining labourers carry out agricultural work. Among them, a distinction must again be made between formal and informal labourers, and between long and short-term contracts. Depending on the activity of the *fazenda*, they can have different tasks, and not all labourers on a *fazenda* work under the regime of *trabalho escravo*.[95]

The largest group of labourers by far are those lowest in the hierarchy, and they are most commonly employed in this labour condition. Their services are only required for physically demanding activities for a limited period of time, mostly for clearing the land and for the harvest.

90 Estreci, *Escravos da desigualdade*: 67.
91 Le Breton, *Vidas roubadas*: 77.
92 Maranhão Costa, "Fighting Forced Labour": 69.
93 Ibid.
94 In Pará, there are 188 rural establishments registered that contain ten thousand hectares or more. Rute Pina, "No Brasil, 2 mil latifúndios ocupam área maior que 4 milhões de propriedades rurais," Brasil de Fato, 26.06.2018, https://www.brasildefato.com.br/2018/07/26/no-brasil-2-mil-latifundios-ocupam-area-maior-que-4-milhoes-de-propriedades-rurais [accessed 03.03.2024].
95 Luana/CPT, Interview 2014.

The labourers carry out their work in teams. These are organised in such a way that there are as few labourers as possible from the same state in the same team, which is meant to reinforce social control. The different teams rarely meet, resulting in the labourers almost only knowing the labourers from their own team. Each team has a team leader, who can be selected either by the *gato* or by the labourers themselves for their communication skills or their age, for example. The team leader works like all other labourers but represents the others in front of the *gato*.[96]

In any case, the labourers doing *trabalho escravo* are constantly other-directed, which means that it is not just about working hard. Their entire rhythm of life is determined by others for months or years. Others determine when and what they eat, when they sleep, when and whether the labourers leave the *fazenda*, and with whom the labourers are allowed to be in contact.

The organisation also depends on the products the *fazenda* produces. In any case, most of the *trabalho escravo* in the agricultural sector and in primary production is done by men. In some production lines, like those for manioc flour, women and men work side by side. In others such as for illegal wood cutting, which is not done on *fazendas* and is therefore differently organised, the labourers come with their families. Some agricultural companies also employ their own cooks, and among them are women, who frequently have to endure *trabalho escravo* too. Women doing *trabalho escravo* are often ignored in the literature, especially in the Amazon region and in the agricultural sector. This also has to do with the activities that have (or are considered to have) the most cases of *trabalho escravo*, with cattle breeding, a mainly masculine activity, still at the top (28 percent for Brazil and 65 percent for Pará between 1995 and 2023).[97]

96 Maranhão Costa, "Fighting Forced Labour": 62–63, 68–69.
97 SmartLab, "Observatório da Erradicação do Trabalho Escravo e do Tráfico de Pessoas."

Coming Out of *trabalho escravo*, Resistance and Brave Escape

In general, there are not a lot of reported instances of organised resistance on the *fazendas*. In contrast to strikes, sabotage is an individual means of resistance that occurs more often.[98] Still, Andreas mentioned a strike that they organised at the Cabaceiras:

> Julia: And did you go on strike to get the attention of the landowner or the government?
> Andreas: [...] The *fazendeiro* didn't live on the *fazenda*. He lived in Belém. It was to get his attention, for him to see our situation, to pay us. We were all at the office door and he arrived and saw a bunch of mango peelings and said: 'What is this?' Then one got up and said: 'It is hunger. We're working, with a formal contract, we are employed. We're starving and in need. And we can't work that way anymore.' Then [...] the *fazendeiro* deposited the money into the account of the farm management, and the farm management paid us. But it never got better. I worked six years on that *fazenda*, all the time in these conditions.[99]

Therefore, the strike in which Andreas participated was only a partial success. In general, the organised resistance of the labourers on the *fazendas* refer to payment and nutrition. It is frequently about alleviating terrible conditions. Fleeing from the *fazenda*, a withdrawal from the conditions, is a personal form of resistance that is also often reported. Some of the fleeing labourers report the *fazendas* to the state authorities in order to free the other labourers.[100] But to be able to flee, the labourers would need a reason as such an escape is extremely dangerous. In a statement to the CPT in Tucumã in 2014, the labourer Luis Fernando, who was hired by a logging company, told his escape story:

---

98 Maranhão Costa, "Fighting Forced Labour": 69–70.
99 Andreas and Maria/MST, Interview 2014.
100 Rezende Figueira, *Pisando fora da própria sombra*: 25.

> The labourers never received [their salary] as agreed and therefore decided to ask to be paid to leave. The farmer told him [Luis Fernando] to leave immediately, in the night, and to go into the woods and disappear. The labourer ran and hid in the woods, and later saw the henchmen looking for him with guns and dogs. When the day dawned, the labourer started to walk into the woods, he walked about 35 km until he found a road, and soon came up against an armed guard, who pointed a gun at Luis Fernando and forced him to return to the *fazenda*. When they got there, Luis Fernando was already humiliated, and he asked to work again out of the fear of being murdered. Then, the *fazendeiro* with his armed guards asked how many days it would take him to finish the job, and the *fazendeiro* told his henchmen, in front of the labourer, to beat the labourer and make him dig a hole and kill him. [...] Then they forced the labourer to get into a pickup truck. During this entire period, the labourer had a gun pointed at his head. While they were walking, they saw the car of another *fazendeiro* with labourers on it. Luis Fernando jumped onto that car in an attempt to escape, but the car was moving slowly as they did not know what was going on. Then, Luis Fernando jumped out again and went into the woods. At this time, the armed guards looked back, chased him into the woods, and shot twice in the direction of the labourer. He dodged and ran faster, ran until he gained distance, and walked again in the woods some 35 km, until he took another road and arrived at a *fazenda*, where he was welcomed and fed [...][101]

An important reason not to flee from *trabalho escravo* is that labourers who are caught are often persecuted and escape is not always successful. Even if they do manage to escape, the labourers often fear being found years later, which sometimes happens. The labourers are also held back by the difficulty of escaping due to the location of the *fazenda* – often in the middle of the Amazonian jungle, sometimes only reachable by airplane – and their lack of knowledge of the region.[102] In most cases,

---

101 Luís Fernando de Amada Conceição, "Declaração. July 17, 2014," CPT Tucumã. English translation from the original in Portuguese by the author.

102 Maranhão Costa, "Fighting Forced Labour": 62, 69.

labourers decide to flee when their lives are threatened. Also, the total lack of food and the labourers realizing that despite working hard, they would never earn anything often lead to the same decision. Humiliation, illness, and poor treatment are also mentioned as reasons for escaping.[103]

As mentioned before, the labour condition does not only end when the labourers escape. In many cases, their contract or task just ends, and they are left somewhere without having realized their aim of earning money. Other labourers who are not held captive, like Andreas or his colleague who was poisoned, just settle their bills and leave on their own account.

Andreas left the Cabaceiras in 1999, and out of fear he never reported the *fazendeiro,* but others did: "Some went to court when they left and went to the Ministry of Labour. They went to court, and they all won the case. They even managed to report it as *trabalho escravo*. [...] Some cases have been confirmed. Because [...] we got sick and there was no assistance, the farm did not provide this assistance."[104] Many labourers on the Cabaceiras did not have a legal contract, even if the labourers had repeatedly been promised one.[105] *Trabalho escravo* was not established for all the labourers, only those whose lives were in acute danger.[106]

The case against the Cabaceiras was enforced through the landless movement (MST) that occupied the *fazenda* in 1999,[107] an organisation that Andreas later joined. In 2014, he and his wife lived on the *acampamento* Hugo Chavez, another squatted *fazenda* in the region around Marabá, not far from the Cabaceiras. Andreas worked somewhere with better labour conditions, and his wife Maria was a cleaner in a school. They had children together and were in high hopes of getting a piece of land through the MST. This probably never happened since the *acampa-*

---

103 Organização Internacional do Trabalho, *Perfil dos principais atores envolvidos no trabalho escravo rural no Brasil:* 38–39.
104 Andreas and Maria/MST, Interview 2014.
105 Barros, "Conquista da Fazenda Cabaceiras."
106 Sakamoto, "Perfil de uma família escravocrata": 31–32.
107 Barros, "O sonho se faz a mão e sem permissão": 18–19.

mento Hugo Chavez is still in dispute,[108] as Marcia, an activist of the CPT in Marabá, recounted in November 2022:

> This area is still in dispute, even today. Because at the time, when they occupied the area, they discovered that part of the farm occupied by the one who claimed to be the owner was public land. [...] So, the people [of the MST] occupied precisely that part. [...] They were evicted once, then they stayed outside and then went back into the area again. But shortly after they returned, they were evicted with great violence. [...] Gunmen and the troops of the *fazendeiro* arrived at the camp at night and started to set it on fire, and the people ran out of the shacks and into the forest. They [the people of the *fazendeiro*] set fire to the houses. Everyone was there. So the people had to run out in the middle of the night. They could just take the children out of the houses, while they [the gunmen] set [everything on] fire. It was very violent. They burned all their belongings. There were people who left with only their clothes on their backs, dragging their children along.[109]

This happened in 2018, and it shows how violent these conflicts around land ownership are. The *fazenda* squatted by the MST is under the self-proclaimed ownership of a member of the Saldanha family, which is, similar to the Mutran family, not only connected to violent land conflicts, but also to *trabalho escravo*.[110] It is unclear what happened to Maria and Andreas after 2014. Following Marcia's statement in 2022, the MST of Marabá was severely decimated because of the violent attacks and out of fear of prospective ones. The difficult situation of different movements defending the rights of the rural labourers and Indigenous people,

108 Daniela Penha and Diego Junqueira, "Aposta de Lula contra a fome, reforma agrária continua parada após 2 meses de governo," MST, 15.03.2023, https://mst.org.br/2023/03/15/aposta-de-lula-contra-a-fome-reforma-agraria-continua-parada-apos-2-meses-de-governo/ [accessed 04.04.2024].

109 Marcia/CPT, Interview by Julia Harnoncourt, 10.11.2022, Marabá.

110 Mauro Ramos, "Pará: Sem terra relatam noite do atentado contra o acampamento Hugo Chávez," Brasil de Fato, 16.08.2018, https://www.brasildefato.com.br/2018/08/16/para-sem-terra-relatam-noite-do-atentado-contra-o-acampamento-hugo-chavez [accessed 30.08.2023].

for example, was aggravated through violence and/or the lack of assets during the Bolsonaro government. This also had a strong influence on the fight against *trabalho escravo*, as even the law against this labour condition and the definition valid today could only come about through social struggles.

Politics and State Mechanisms in the Fight Against *trabalho escravo*

Before the introduction of laws and mechanisms against *trabalho escravo*, it was primarily the labourers' families who searched for their family members and fought, together with the labourers, to get people out of those labour conditions. Also, social movements tried to draw public attention to the problem, at first only on a case by case basis. Systematic campaigns and efforts to make *trabalho escravo* visible began only in 1975 with the struggles of the Pastoral Land Commission (CPT).[111] One of the most important early cases that received widespread attention was the case of the Volkswagen-*fazenda* Rio Cristalino in Pará, which was first reported for *trabalho escravo* in 1983. Further complaints were then raised against the company. Social movements and organisations worked together to publicise this case both in Brazil and in Europe. As back then there was no legal framework against *trabalho escravo*, it was only in 2022 that the Brazilian public prosecutor's office entered into negotiations with Volkswagen regarding the compensations of the labourers, a claim that was rejected by the company the following year.[112]

Another case involving the international public that was crucial for the development of the legislation against *trabalho escravo* is the already-mentioned case of José Pereira. He worked together with sixty other labourers on the *fazenda* Espírito Santo in southern Pará, under the

[111] De Souza Martins, "The Reappearance of Slavery and the Reproduction of Capital on the Brazilian Frontier": 282.

[112] Christian Russau, "Sklavenarbeit auf der VW-Fazenda Rio Cristalino in Amazonien," https://www.kooperation-brasilien.org/de/themen/menschenrechte-gesellschaft/sklavenarbeit-auf-der-vw-fazenda-rio-cristalino-in-amazonien [accessed 11.07.2023].

labour regime that later became known as *trabalho escravo*. The *fazenda* Espírito Santo was also owned by a member of the Mutran family. José Pereira and another labourer tried to escape in 1989. They were caught and shot at. While Pereira was able to flee, his companion died. Five years later, a group of social organisations reported the case to the Organization of American States (OAS). According to the OAS, the state was negligent and failed to protect its citizen José Pereira from "slavery" and bodily harm, which made it an accomplice to those conditions. The state was also accused of not showing interest and being inefficient in investigating the case. The government finally had to recognize its responsibility, which led to the introduction of the laws against *trabalho escravo* in 1995.[113]

At the time, the law defined the condition only through the immobilization of the labourers, for example, through force or threat. The first state mechanisms and laws to combat this employment were introduced in the same year. They were mainly about the liberation of the labourers and the punishment of the entrepreneurs. An important mechanism was the Mobile Inspection Group (*Grupo Especial de Fiscalização Móvel*/GEFM), established to conduct labour inspections, to investigate allegations of *trabalho escravo* on the ground, to free labourers, and to initiate prosecutions.[114] While at the beginning labourers reported *trabalho escravo* mostly to local organisations, like labour unions or the CPT, for example, who forwarded the complaints to the GEFM, the process later became easier and today, it can be done via the Internet, which is widely used.

In 2003, as already mentioned, the definition of *trabalho escravo* was amplified, and exhaustive workdays (*jornadas exaustivas*) and degrading conditions (*condições degradantes*) were added to the legal definition, which already included the immobilization of the labourers. As explained by Xavier Plassat, the coordinator of the CPT's campaign against *trabalho escravo*, this amplification was a result of the practice

113 Harnoncourt and Paredes, "Theorizing Human Trafficking"; Sakamoto, "Perfil de uma família escravocrata": 32.

114 Aurélie Hauchere Vuong, "A Multidisciplinary Approach to Combat Forced Labour – Lessons Learned from Brazil," *Global Eye on Human Trafficking* 12 (2013): 1.

in the labour inspections.[115] Violating the law should be punishable by two to eight years in prison and a fine. Normally, the fine is calculated based on the withheld wages and benefits, the cost of the inspection, and the damage to society, as it is assumed that the use of *trabalho escravo* is not only harmful to the labourers themselves, but also to society as a whole.[116] Even though the fines are often imposed, the imprisonment of entrepreneurs rarely happens.

Another important tool for fighting *trabalho escravo* was added in 2004: the "dirty list" (*lista suja*). On this list the names of entrepreneurs penalized for employing *trabalho escravo* are made public for two years, which has broad consequences regarding business partners and creditworthiness. It is quite an effective measure, which is why it is also highly disputed. In 2014, through the political intervention of a group of construction companies, the *lista suja* was deferred for about two years. Fortunately, the list has been reactivated, even if there are still attempts to invalidate it, as Xavier Plassat mentioned in 2022:

> Today, the *lista suja* is being brutally attacked; not the *lista suja* itself, but they [the entrepreneurs] are creating instruments in order to avoid getting on the *lista suja*. One of the most revolting cases that we have just seen is that of one of the main construction companies in Brazil called MRV.[117] It has already had, if not five, then eight cases of *trabalho escravo* over the last ten years, and it was on the *lista suja*. It has already been placed on the *lista suja* and has now obtained the court decision to be taken off it.[118]

115 Plassat/CPT, Interview 2014.

116 De Castro Gomes, "Repression and Changes in Slave-Like Labor in Brazil": 122–23.

117 Daniel Camargos, "Após 7 flagrantes, MRV é beneficiada por acordo com governo e fica fora da 'lista suja' do trabalho escravo," Repórter Brasil, 28.10.2022, https://reporterbrasil.org.br/2022/10/apos-7-flagrantes-mrv-e-beneficiada-por-acordo-com-governo-e-fica-fora-da-lista-suja-do-trabalho-escravo/ [accessed 30.08.2023]; "MRV," https://www.mrv.com.br/ [accessed 04.04.2024].

118 Xavier Plassat/CPT, Interview by Julia Harnoncourt, 07.11.2022, Araguaína.

This is, as Xavier Plassat stated, problematic, as the possibility of applying pressure to be taken off the list, especially that exerted by powerful and wealthy enterprises, damages its effectiveness.

While these laws and mechanisms were established either under the government of Fernando Henrique Cardoso of the social democratic party (PSDB), who was president from 1993 to 2003, or under Luiz Inácio Lula da Silva of the labour party (PT), president from 2003 to 2011 and again from 2023 to the present, no new improvements have been made, with the political shift in the recent years.

Dilma Rousseff, also from the PT, became president in 2011 and was re-elected in 2014. In December 2015, however, a process of impeachment started, which was initiated in the wake of allegations of corruption against the entire government; it was known as *Lava-Jato*. In April 2016, Rousseff was removed from office, and an interim government under right-wing President Michel Temer was installed, whose members were also later affected by the corruption allegations. This was possible as the power within Brazil had shifted towards the landowning elites, which could be seen through the increased influence of the representatives of the landowners and agribusinesses in parliament and in legislative assemblies (*bancada ruralista*). Even though the Brazilian Labour Party never questioned the economic development project or changed the basic power structure while in office, they still managed to introduce and strengthen social programs, and to make improvements to the labour law. The interim government, on the other hand, cut social benefits and curtailed constitutional rights within a few months of assuming power, especially those of the Indigenous population and labourers.[119] Although the laws and mechanisms against *trabalho escravo* were not directly altered, changes that would influence their efficacy were made, for example, through the introduction of the labour reform and outsourcing law in 2017.[120] Natalia Suzuki, a journalist of *Repórter Brasil*,

[119] Ivan Hegenberg, "Aspectos subjectivos de nossa crise política," Le Monde Diplomatique Brasil, 02.10.2015, https://diplomatique.org.br/aspectos-subjetivos-de-nossa-crise-politica/ [accessed 30.08.2023].

[120] "Entenda o projeto de lei da terceirização aprovado pela Câmara," Agencia Brasil, https://agenciabrasil.ebc.com.br/economia/noticia/2017-03/entenda-o-projeto-de-lei-da-terceirizacao-aprovado-pela-camara [accessed 08.08.2023]; "Reforma

an NGO that aims to identify and publish violations of labour rights, later confirmed this:

> The biggest difficulty is that the labour legislation as a whole was changed. People cannot forget that *trabalho escravo* is part of the world of labour. It is not a separate category. So, when the labour legislation is reformulated, as was done in 2017 by the Temer government, this has significant impacts on the issue of *trabalho escravo*. Why? Because [...] you allow the flexibility of contracts, you allow the precariousness of labourer activities, of working conditions, which were legally not allowed before. And the bar, the standards that we have, so that we could guarantee decent labour, are lowered. Therefore, forms that we did not consider possible, regular, or permissible in the world of labour end up being allowed, situations of exploitation that before we didn't think would be possible now end up being regulated, in this logic of the labour reform.[121]

In 2019, the far-right politician Jair Messias Bolsonaro, then member of the Social Liberal Party (PSL), became president. Under his presidency, the labour law was made even more flexible, until it became, for specific types of contracts, nearly only based upon an agreement between employer and employee, which is an extremely dangerous condition in the context of *trabalho escravo*.[122]

Bolsonaro is the most criticized Brazilian president since the democratization of the country. He delivered an anti-environmentalist and anti-Indigenous discourse, defended gun ownership, and saw the rise of poverty and inequality during his presidency.[123] After his presidency

---

trabalhista completa um ano sob questionamentos e sem desfecho," Senadonoticias, 09.09.2018, https://www12.senado.leg.br/noticias/materias/2018/11/09/reforma-trabalhista-completa-um-ano-sob-questionamentos-e-sem-desfecho [accessed 10.08.2023].

121 Natália Suzuki/Reporter Brasil, Interview by Julia Harnoncourt, 18.08.2022. Zoom.

122 Marcia/CPT, Interview 2022; Julia Neves, "Carteira de trabalho verde e amarela: entenda seu funcionamento," oitchau, 28.06.2023, https://www.oitchau.com.br/blog/carteira-de-trabalho-verde-e-amarela-entenda-seu-funcionamento/ [accessed 30.08.2023].

123 Henri Acselrad, "A Amazônia e o antiambientalismo de resultados," Le Monde Diplomatique Brasil, 12.08.2020, https://diplomatique.org.br/a-amazonia-e-o-antiambi-

ended, Bolsonaro was incriminated in judicial cases regarding the abuse of power and misuse of media outlets. He was also accused of spreading misinformation about COVID, of decimating the Indigenous population, and of deforestation, which nearly doubled during his presidency.[124] Regarding *trabalho escravo*, the biggest problems that my interview partners mentioned were the cutting of funds and the decrease in support for the mechanisms that fight against this labour condition. They also pointed to problems with the discourse and the increase in impunity regarding *trabalho escravo*, the violence on the countryside, and the violation of Indigenous rights, inter alia. As Xavier Plassat of the CPT-Brazil mentioned in 2022:

> There was, with the Bolsonaro years or even shortly before, a reduction in the resources available to combat *trabalho escravo*, and a constant delegitimization of the environmental or labour inspections by the government. [...] At the same time [there was] a discourse of total liberalization of deforestation, mining exploitation in Indigenous territories, and a complete paralysis of the agrarian reform and of the recognition

---

entalismo-de-resultados/ [accessed 30.08.2023]; Gleber César Buzatto, "O governo Bolsonaro e o anticonstitucionalismo contra os povos indígenas," Le Monde Diplomatique Brasil, 22.01.2019, https://diplomatique.org.br/o-governo-bolsonaro-e-o-anti-constitucionalismo-contra-os-povos-indigenas/ [accessed 13.07.2023]; Patricia Fachin, "Plano mais Brasil não é um projeto de crescimento, mas de aprofundamento da desigualdade econômica e social. Entrevista especial com Guilherme Delgado," https://www.ihu.unisinos.br/categorias/159-entrevistas/594272-plano-mais-brasil-nao-e-um-projeto-de-crescimento-mas-de-aprofundamento-da-desigualdade-economica-e-social-entrevista-especial-com-guilherme-delgado?gclid=EAIaIQobChMInOzjwtGd_AIVKexcCh0thwUjEAMYASAAEgJPpPD_BwE [accessed 13.07.2023].

124 Ricardo Brito and Gabriel Araujo, "Bolsonaro barred from Holding Public Office in Brazil until 2030," Reuters, 01.06.2023, https://www.reuters.com/world/americas/political-career-brazils-bolsonaro-dangles-by-thread-electoral-trial-nears-end-2023-06-30/ [accessed 08.08.2023]; Anthony Boadle and Lisandra Paraguassu, "Satellite Data Shows Amazon Deforestation Rising under Brazil's Bolsonaro," Reuters, 04.06.2019, https://www.reuters.com/article/us-brazil-environment-deforestation-idUSKCN1T52OQ [accessed 30.08.2023]; "Jair Bolsonaro Accused of Inciting Genocide before the International Criminal Court," Open Democracy, 29.11.2029, https://www.opendemocracy.net/en/democraciaabierta/jair-bolsonaro-accused-inciting-genocide-international-criminal-court/ [accessed 30.08.2023]; Florence Davey-Attlee, "Brazil's Bolsonaro Accused of Crimes against Humanity at ICC for His Record on the Amazon," CNN, 12.10.2021, https://edition.cnn.com/2021/10/12/americas/brazil-bolsonaro-icc-crimes-against-humanity-intl/index.html [accessed 30.08.2023].

> of Indigenous territories. So, all of this is a context that sends a firm and constant message to agribusinesses: 'You are free to do whatever you want in this country.' So, an extremely favourable environment, we can say, to multiply the cases of *trabalho escravo*.[125]

But as Natalia Suzuki of the Repórter Brasil insisted, this development, the neglect of the fight against *trabalho escravo*, already began during the government of Dilma Rousseff (2011–2016):

> There is no budget, little budget for inspections, there are no posts for labour inspectors [...]. There is no equipment for inspections, it is increasingly precarious. [...] At the same time, the issue of post-rescue policy, coordinated at the state level, [...] is also deprived on several fronts. But I want to be fair here, because we always think that the problem started with Temer and got worse with the Bolsonaro government, which is a big lie, because the problem was already there during the Dilma government. [...] The problem of *trabalho escravo* was no longer a priority during the Dilma government. It never was. During the Dilma government, this issue was negotiated on so many fronts that I no longer remember. There was the question of the suspension of the *lista suja*. [...] We already had very serious problems with regard to labour inspectors. The problems with these inspections have been going on since 2010. So, it is not new, it is not the Bolsonaro government, it stems from before.[126]

Therefore, even before today, there was already a lack of labour inspectors, especially in Pará, and there have never been sufficient programs to fight against the precariousness and poverty of the labourers enticed by the *gatos* – a situation that drives them into *trabalho escravo*. And as Natalia Suzuki said, effective countrywide programs for labourers rescued from this labour condition have never existed. Therefore, even the labourers freed by the GEFM would find themselves in the same precari-

125 Plassat/CPT, Interview 2022.
126 Suzuki/Reporter Brasil, Interview 2022.

ous position as before entering *trabalho escravo*, at least in Pará. As long as there are that many labourers willing to enter such labour relations, because they have no alternatives, this system will probably not disappear.

Of course, the lack of funds for the labour inspections, as well as the general political situation, has had an impact on the inspections themselves, as Carlos, a labour inspector in Pará, recounted in 2023:

> The inspections of *trabalho escravo* started in 1995, but they got stronger from 2003, 2004 onwards, because the government from then on was a government with a little stronger social focus, and it was concerned with these issues. And there was an increase in the funds and per diems [...] The labour inspections intensified, and the legislation became a little stricter. [...] This made the landowners more aware of it [*trabalho escravo*]. So, labour inspections increased, the law was stricter, and there was a drop [in *trabalho escravo*]. [...] But in 2018, the federal government itself weakened this. [...] It used a discourse to minimize, criticize some infraction notices. The chief executive [meaning then-President Bolsonaro] criticised some infraction notices to disturb the labour inspectors. [...] Cutting funds, the involvement in the labour inspections, the armament discourse – all of this made us move away a little because we no longer felt safe; it was no longer a matter of legal security, we no longer felt physically safe in carrying out an inspection.[127]

All of this caused the number of inspections to drop, at least in Pará, a fact that is also true for the whole northern region (all of which forms part of the Amazon region). The diagram below shows how the number of inspected businesses in Pará rose in the 2000s, with a first peak in 2003 and a second one in 2010, only to drop later. Brazil as a whole shows another picture, as the number of inspected businesses has been rising recently.[128]

[127] Carlos/inspetor do trabalho, Interview by Julia Harnoncourt, 10.01.2023, Webex.
[128] Comissão Pastoral da Terra, "Panorama atualizado do trabalho escravo no Brasil: coleção e análise de dados" [accessed 26.08.2023, sent via email 30.06.2022].

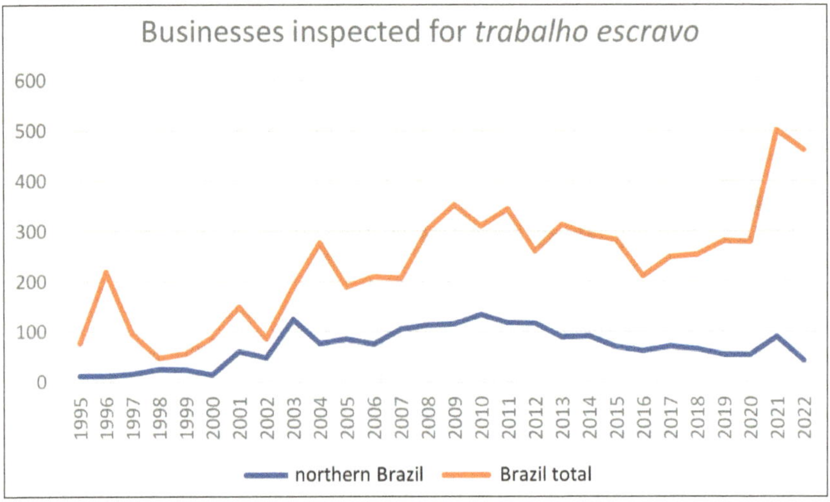

This divergence could have different reasons: Some interviewees stated that in spite of the drop in funds, there has been a lot of personal engagement on the part of the labour inspectors in other states, which increased the numbers for Brazil. A reason for the drop in numbers in the northern region could be the infrastructural difficulties encountered in the Amazon jungle, which are even harder to overcome with a lack of funds, especially regarding the inspection of some locations, where helicopters are needed. Another reason could be the unequal distribution of funds inside Brazil since the decentralization of the GEFM, as the northern regions are Brazil's peripheries that have always been disadvantaged.[129] What it definitely does not mean is that *trabalho escravo* in Pará is on the decline. Carlos, the labour inspector from that state, mentioned that they have many reports of *trabalho escravo* that they cannot even follow up:

> Especially because the last four years [...] we were almost extinct. [...] There was a shortage of funds in fiscal planning and action, Julia. That was deliberate. It was not because the country was going through a cri-

[129] Carlos/inspetor do trabalho, Interview 2023; Plassat/CPT, Interview 2022; Jônatas Andrade, Interview by Julia Harnoncourt, 28.10.2022, Webex; Ricardo Rezende Figueira, Interview by Julia Harnoncourt, 17.11.2022, Aracajú.

> sis. Before the pandemic, it already happened. [...] Notably, an attempt was made to prevent the [labour] actions from taking place. The caucus that was in power for the last four years, not only in the legislative, but also in the executive, the *bancada ruralista* – it is very strong in Brazil. So, they did everything to minimize it [the fight against *trabalho escravo*...]. Labour inspections in Pará have diminished a lot. [...] The signs were already there shortly before the 2018 election, as the former president [Bolsonaro] was strongly linked to the agribusiness [...] He defended the armament because of the issue of the safety of the agribusiness personnel. The justification then was a matter of personal safety and private property. We now experience more threats [...] From then on [after they were threatened with weapons], we started to carry out our actions only when accompanied by the police force. We didn't do it with the police before. [...] And this reduces the number of inspections a lot, because when we were alone with our drivers doing the inspections, we didn't need a lot of bureaucracy. When you call the police, there's a whole process, there's a whole coordination, a daily rate, displacement...[130]

So, apart from the lack of funds and the conditions of the Amazon region, labour inspectors also suffer violent threats, which makes their inspections more complicated as they need to be accompanied by the police for personal safety. Another reason might be a change in the sectors the labour inspectorate is interested in.

Possible Shifts in the System of *trabalho escravo*

It seems that the labour inspectorate has broadened their scope, going beyond cattle and sugar cane and now looking into other agricultural products. In Pará, where cattle raising made 66 percent of labourers in cattle raising were freed from *trabalho escravo* between 1995 and 2018, while the same sector saw only a total of 38 percent of labourers freed

---

130 Carlos/inspetor do trabalho, Interview 2023.

between 2018 and 2022, followed by metal extraction (29 percent) and something called "native forest" (10 percent).[131] It should be underlined that the existing numbers are a result of the labour inspections. What they reflect is therefore a mix of different factors: the existence of *trabalho escravo* in the different states of Brazil and the economic sectors, the interests of the labour inspectorate as well as changes in business strategies. So, it is unclear if the use of *trabalho escravo* itself shifted toward other sectors, or if it is just the inspections that did. In any case, the scope of my interviewees shifted toward the same direction. In contrast to 2014, where mainly cattle, charcoal production, and sometimes soy plantations were mentioned in the interviews, a lot of different sectors were discussed in 2022, as Marcia from the CPT in Marabá did in our interview:

> Cattle breeding is still on the rise, because in fact it is an area that employs the most labourers due to the great extensions of land they have. [...] Another segment that has appeared is related to this issue of extractivism, the issue of [the] açai [berry][132], which is something that is increasing a lot [...] in the region of Belém, the region of Marajó. [...] People are enslaved in wood cutting, then there is the issue of palm oil. [...] We have already seen it, too, in the production of cocoa, not with much expressiveness, but it exists in cocoa cultivation, [...] in palm hearts production, too.[133]

As mentioned before, mining has been on the rise, so much so that labour judge Jônatas Andrade speaks of the "emergence of a new profile of *trabalho escravo*".[134] Here, it might be interesting to know that in the 2000s, *trabalho escravo* was already extensively being used in the production of charcoal for the iron industry, which later declined because

131 SmartLab, "Observatório da Erradicação do Trabalho Escravo e do Tráfico de Pessoas."
132 The açai berry is the fruit of a palm tree native to the Amazon region. In the Amazon region it is eaten in the form of a puree, often as a side dish for fish. It can also be eaten in the form of a desert. It is very nutritious and is considered a "super fruit" in western countries today. Açai oil is a further use of the plant.
133 Marcia/CPT, Interview 2022.
134 Andrade, Interview 2022.

the parts where charcoal was needed had been outsourced. Today, *trabalho escravo* can be found in small-scale mining, mainly for gold. In this sector, the small enterprises often work without permits and with nearly no mechanization, which is why they need more manual labour. Gold in Pará is mostly found along the river Tapajós, with the city of Itaituba being one of the biggest hubs for illegal mining in Brazil. The city's whole economy is driven by and geared towards the gold business – a concentration that only intensified with the advent of the Bolsonaro administration as, especially during this time, the president himself supported the political mining lobby.[135] The region seems to be marked by violence in general. Xavier Plassat, for example, recounted that the CPT wanted to launch a program there but was discouraged because "the threats of violence were tremendous".[136] Furthermore, big parts of this area have been assigned to Indigenous groups, mostly the Munduruku. But even these areas are illegally invaded by mining companies, who do not only pollute the waters, but also cause violent conflicts. In these conflicts, many Indigenous leaders are murdered,[137] as Mauricio Torres, an expert on the Amazon jungle at the University of Pará, confirmed in an interview in 2022: "Here in eastern Pará, we have the Munduruku women, for example. They put up great resistance – not for the land, but for the territory – against the mining industry. And now they are threatened, they suffer violence. One of their great leaders, Maria Eleusa, had her house burned down. It's an absurdly violent thing."[138]

A connection between the illegal mining sector and drug trafficking as well as prostitution can also be made. Pará is the state that has the

[135] Maya Johnson, "$200 Million in Gold Extracted in Amazon Mine through Illegal Licenses," Mongabay, 25.10.2021, https://news.mongabay.com/2021/10/200-million-in-gold-extracted-in-amazon-mine-through-illegal-licenses/ [accessed 31.08.2023]; Luisa Molina and Luiz J. Wanderley, *O cerco do ouro: garimpo ilegal, destruição e luta em terras Munduruku* (Brasilia: Comitê Nacional em Defesa dos Territórios Frente à Mineração, 2021).

[136] Plassat/CPT, Interview 2022

[137] Johnson, "$200 Million in Gold Extracted in Amazon Mine through Illegal Licenses"; Fabiola Perez, "Ações do PCC fortalecem permanência de garimpeiros na Terra Yanomami," UOL, 03.05.2023, https://noticias.uol.com.br/cotidiano/ultimas-noticias/2023/05/03/pcc-acao-garimpeiros-terra-indigena-yanomami.htm [accessed 31.08.2023].

[138] Mauricio Torres, Interview by Julia Harnoncourt, 20.12.2022, Whatsapp.

highest number of labourers freed from *trabalho escravo* in the mining sector.[139] Even though the small-scale businesses form part of a bigger network of production/distribution, it is only they who are held accountable. Their buyers, the big businesses, succeed in not being discovered.[140]

The third biggest activity in Pará where *trabalho escravo* has recently been identified is in the cutting of noble woods in the native forests of the Amazon region. Xavier Plassat of the CPT already knew about this activity in 2014. But its extension was probably not clear back then since labour as well as environmental inspections only began in 2015:[141]

> Behind the frontier [of capitalist extension…] we have the information that there is *trabalho escravo*. But it is covered up by clandestinity. Selective wood cutting, selective deforestation, operates very differently from the past, in a criminal climate, which causes the population involved to be afraid to denounce it, because it would be exposing themselves to being murdered. This is a situation that ends up being maintained without anyone denouncing it and with a lot of connivance. So, this situation is typical of Pará and the interior of the Amazon.[142]

What Xavier Plassat described is still true today. This sector cuts noble woods in small-scale dimensions in the middle of the jungle, which makes these operations harder to find than, for example, cattle-raising *fazendas*, which work on big extensions of land. Most of those woodcutting enterprises are found along the highway BR-163. It is not only the gold mining companies, but also the woodcutting companies that are

139 Bansal et al, "An Intervention-Focused Review of Modern Slave Labor in Brazil's Mining Sector"; Mauricio Angelo, "Trabalho escravo em garimpos expõe redes criminosas na Amazônia," Mongabay, 11.02.2021, https://brasil.mongabay.com/2021/02/trabalho-escravo-em-garimpos-expoe-redes-criminosas-na-amazonia/ [accessed 12.08.2023]; Sam Cowie, "A bordo de uma balsa de garimpo: quanto vale a vida no mercado de ouro ilegal?" Repórter Brasil, 13.09.2021, https://reporterbrasil.org.br/2021/09/a-bordo-de-uma-balsa-de-garimpo-quanto-vale-a-vida-no-mercado-de-ouro-ilegal/ [accessed 16.08.2023].

140 Plassat/CPT, Interview 2022.

141 CDVDH/CB, CPT, *Por debaixo da Floresta*: 18.

142 Plassat/CPT, Interview 2014.

involved with organised crime, extorting and threatening the local communities in order to obtain their complicity or at least connivance.[143] In woodcutting, there is normally a production chain involved that uses outsourcing. The bigger enterprises, the logging companies, buy their wood from a sawmill. The sawmill hires a *toreiro*, a person who, like the *gato,* organises the labourers that would cut the wood. The *toreiro* normally comes from the same social strata as the labourers and is also always indebted – to the sawmill, to the fuel and other equipment merchants, sometimes to friends and relatives, as well as to his labourers. Even though the wood is cut in protected areas and is therefore illegal, the companies manage to present the wood as legal through different elaborate schemes, sometimes involving state officials, while going through the production chain. Mauricio Torres from the University of Pará, who was involved in a book project on the topic,[144] also reported on the supply chains of these operations:

> This wood […] is the most precious wood. This wood is basically exported [… to] the United States and Europe. The logging companies here in Belém export all over the world. […] I explain in the book that the outsourcing reveals exploitation in *condições análogas de escravidão* (conditions analogous to slavery [legal term]).[145]

In woodcutting, the labourers freed from *trabalho escravo*, in contrast to other sectors, are mostly locals, sometimes Indigenous people, as their knowledge about the jungle is important. Because of their poor living conditions in the southeast of Pará, with no infrastructure and a lack of schools and health services, for example, they can be pressured into these working conditions. As they are accustomed to hard labour without any rights and to precarious living situations, they often regard the conditions in doing *trabalho escravo* in the woodcutting sector as normal,

143 Plassat/CPT, Interview 2022; CDVDH/CB, CPT, *Por debaixo da Floresta.*
144 CDVDH/CB, CPT, *Por debaixo da Floresta.*
145 Torres, Interview 2022.

even though many labourers have died or have been mutilated while doing that activity.[146]

My interviewees furthermore stressed the existence of *trabalho escravo* in the production of different crops, which made up around 9 percent of the labourers freed from this labour regime in Pará between 2018 and 2023.[147] One of the crops mentioned is the dendê palm, whose fruits are used to make oil. On these plantations, those who work in *trabalho escravo* are mainly men.[148] Another product is açai, which is, as Marcia of the CPT Marabá mentioned, a staple food for the people of Pará, but also used for export:

> The açai here in the region is already used for export. It goes to the big cities, to the big capitals, to Rio de Janeiro, São Paulo, Brazil and beyond. [...] So that is why the açai oil around here is very expensive. Açai is the food base of the people of the riverside, [...] of the Indigenous people, of the people who have more contact with the forest. [...] It is from Pará. I still don't know of any other state that is producing it for large exports.[149]

The products of *trabalho escravo*, therefore, are not only found in the Brazilian market, but also in the world market. This is not only true for açai; it is also true for noble woods and for dendê and other palm oil, as well as for beef and for oranges used in orange juice production. Regarding the latter two products, Brazil is one of their biggest producers.[150] As mentioned by my interview partners in 2022, orange production,

146 CDVDH/CB, CPT, *Por debaixo da Floresta.*

147 SmartLab, "Observatório da Erradicação do Trabalho Escravo e do Tráfico de Pessoas."

148 Ângela Conceição Lopes de Jesus/presidenta FETAGRI-PA, Interview by Julia Harnoncourt, 04.11.2022, Belem.

149 Marcia/CPT, Interview 2022.

150 "Brazil Is the World's Fourth Largest Grain Producer and Top Beef Exporter, Study Shows," Embrapa 50, June 1, 2021, https://www.embrapa.br/en/busca-de-noticias/-/noticia/62619259/brazil-is-the-worlds-fourth-largest-grain-producer-and-top-beef-exporter-study-shows [accessed 31.08.2023]; CDVDH/CB, CPT, *Por debaixo da Floresta*: 38; Flora Southey, "More Trees, Less Land: How Brazil's Orange Juice Sector Trippled Its Productivity," FoodNavigator, 09.10.2022, https://www.foodnavigator.com/Article/2022/12/09/Densification-How-Brazil-s-orange-juice-sector-produces-more-with-less [accessed 31.08.2023].

among many other products, involves the use of *trabalho escravo*. Carlos, the labour inspector who then went deeper into *trabalho escravo* in flour production, also spoke of this:

> Then we find *trabalho escravo* in orange production. And this happens in palm oil, in black pepper production. It is very common in black pepper production. They even use children. We find it in flour production. [...] The production of flour is a basic artisanal production, and it is very complicated to determine *trabalho análogo à escravidão* (labour analogous to slavery) in flour production because they do not think they are in this condition. They think they are working in a family farming system. In practice, they are not. [...] Because behind them there are the owners of the machines that are exploiting the work of women and children. [...] With flour [...] it's not that the owner is a big producer. He is not. Sometimes he is working there together with the labourers. But since he owns the means of production, he owns the machines, he has a little more means than the others, he ends up recruiting [labourers]. [...] We find a lot of situations similar to *trabalho análogo à escravidão* (labour analogous to slavery): We find children, women, in degrading conditions, working on the ground, in the mud, peeling manioc – peeling it, pressing it into flour, working in very high temperatures under a shed. But in their conception, it is something normal, natural, because that's how flour is produced. But that is not how it's done.[151]

Apart from the different sectors where *trabalho escravo* is used, Carlos also addresses two other topics: (1) the normalization of this labour condition; but also, and this might be new in agriculture, (2) *trabalho escravo* in small-scale and even family-based businesses, or in the form of a supposed self-employment. Supposed self-employment is a form of labour organisation that has been mentioned by many of my interview partners as a new form of organising and veiling *trabalho escravo*. It corresponds with a general shift in organising the production process, from the centralized production under one brand to ever smaller pseudo-autonomous

[151] Carlos/inspetor do trabalho, Interview 2023.

units outsourced in production chains. Ricardo Rezende Figueira, a priest, human rights activist, professor at the Federal University of Rio de Janeiro, and expert on the topic of *trabalho escravo*, confirmed this in relation to chicken rearing:

> If you take, for example, Sadia[152], which sells chicken – until the 1980s, it had sheds […], it raised the chickens, then it killed the chickens, froze the chickens, sold the chickens. What did it do? It dismantled this shed where it raised the chickens, and the small owners now buy the chick from Sadia, buy food for the chick, and sell the [grown] chicken to Sadia. So, they first pay for the chick and the food, and then sell the chicken. If there is a disease, the chickens die, [but] Sadia has no loss because the chicken does not belong to it.[153]

Legally and theoretically, how is it then possible to determine *trabalho escravo*? Where is the line between self-employment or self-exploitation and the responsibilities of the manufacturer, retailer, or brand? And which actor(s) should be made responsible and to what extent? These are for sure important and interesting questions, which might be too broad to answer here. Regarding *trabalho escravo*, and following the law, debt bondage serves as the main indicator here. Feliz, a member of the CPT in Tucuruí, explained this using the example of chestnut gathering:

> For example, Adriana has a business. And at her shop, she sells clothes, food products, shoes – in short, everything you need is there at Adriana's shop. I work with chestnuts […]. She will advise me on what I need to harvest chestnuts, to extract chestnuts, to cut chestnuts, gather them. Then she will provide me with rice, sugar, coffee, a hat, clothes, boots, a machete. […] Then I'm forced to sell the nuts that I cut, that I gather, only to her – for the price she wants to pay me. […] Then it may be that all my nuts won't be enough to pay for the boots, the machete,

152 Sadia, https://www.sadia.com.br/ [accessed 31.08.2023].
153 Rezende Figueira, Interview 2022.

> the rice, the beans, the oil, the work clothes that I got, that she lent me. I'm going to deliver all my chestnuts and I'm still going to be in debt, forced to find other jobs to pay what I owe.[154]

In another interview with Feliz in 2022, he went deeper into the debt mechanisms and how debt could be maintained, this time based on fishing activities:

> For example, today the price of peacock bass is 10 reais a kilo, and then the fisherman goes fishing. If he arrives with a large volume of peacock bass, he [the person who lent him the fishing materials] lowers the price of peacock bass from 10, sometimes even to 3 reais, precisely so that the fisherman [...] would continue to not make a profit and continue to owe his creditor.[155]

This system has not only been mentioned in relation to fishing and chestnut gathering, but also to the production of charcoal and in the form of a pyramid scheme, where the victims of debt bondage become labour recruiters as well. As Marcia mentioned in 2022, under this scheme, the participants have to sell the products in the streets.[156]

Political Power Struggles: *Trabalho escravo* and Other Issues

In the preceding sections, it could already be seen how the power struggles, mainly those inside the realm of official state politics, influence the fight against *trabalho escravo*. But also how big landowners, entrepreneurs, and their interest groups, as well as social and grassroots movements that deal with the rights of precarious populations, influence the state. The first group influences the state on two levels: on a small-scale and local level, and on the national level. Many politicians represent their interests, for example, through the *bancada ruralista* in the National

[154] Feliz and Jamiro/CPT, Interview by Julia Harnoncourt, 09.11.2022, Tucuruí.
[155] Grupo RAICE, Interview by Julia Harnoncourt, 10.11.2022, Itupiranga.
[156] Marcia/CPT, Interview 2022.

Congress. In the majority of cases, the courts also side with the powerful group. After all, many politicians and judges own large estates themselves. For this reason, Thays, the coordinator of the *Centro da Defesa da Vida e Dos Direitos Humanos Carmen Bascaran* (CDVDH), came to this conclusion as early as 2014:

> I think the government is a very big instrument, and it doesn't depend on the president alone. It depends on the politics in general, which, most of the time, is full of people who also feed *trabalho escravo*. So how to combat it? If the same person who practices it is the same person who should fight it?[157]

At the local level, such as in Pará, in the interior of the Amazon region, *fazendeiros* do not influence an existing government but rather exercise direct power, often with great violence.[158] This happens due to the lack of state power in some regions, as Pará is spacious and has many areas that are difficult to access due to the jungle. When state institutions do exist, officials are often bribed or threatened so that the local and personal power of the old or new elites is maintained.[159]

As we have seen in the history of the laws against *trabalho escravo*, as well as through the statements of my interview partners, social and grassroots movements are also involved in the fight against this labour condition to an important degree. How much their opinions are considered again depends on the distribution of power inside the government. During the Bolsonaro government, social movements were actively impeded or even fought against. Angela Conceição Lopes de Jesus, director of the FETAGRI-PA, the section of the labour union representing agricultural labourers, accounted for this in 2022:

---

[157] Thays/CDVDH, Interview by Julia Harnoncourt, 26.11.2014, Araguaína.

[158] Le Breton, *Vidas roubadas*: 78, 227; Centro de Documentação Dom Tomás Balduino, ed., "Conflitos no Campo: Brasil 2022," Goiânia, 2023.

[159] Rezende Figueira, "A Persistência da Escravidão Ilegal no Brasil": 62.

> Our worst moment, I tell you, was during the Bolsonaro government. [...] We had a lot of difficulties because of the problem of criminalizing social movements. [...] So, this also repressed the movement a little, put the leaders of the agricultural labourers in a difficult situation. [...] Not to mention that agribusiness was not idle at all: the acquisition of weapons, invasion of land, deforestation – all in favour of soy and cattle.[160]

But it was not only criminalization that slowed down the social and grassroots movements: Based on the accounts of the labour inspector or about the MST, the spike in violence, at least in Pará, is connected to the "erosion of rights", as labour judge Jônatas Andrade called it.[161] Furthermore, the lack of funding also caused, inter alia, a lack of personnel, which was strikingly visible during my research in November 2022. This, of course, also influenced the fight against *trabalho escravo*.[162]

The struggles related to *trabalho escravo* are also connected to other political fields, like general labour conditions, violence in the countryside, land ownership, protection of the environment, the rainforest, and Indigenous communities, but also to racism and gender roles and the intersection of all of these topics. In most of these fields, my interview partners all stood in opposition to the Bolsonaro government, as did, for example, Feliz of the CPT in Tucuruí in 2022: "It [Bolsonaro's government] is a government that messes up the environmental laws, the labour laws, and opens the doors for cattle breeding [...]. There are several Indians, Indigenous leaders, that have been murdered – labourers murdered, labourers evicted, illegally arrested."[163]

Feliz also mentioned the great violence with which land conflicts were brought about. Disputes over land were not new to the Bolsonaro government, but rather go back to as early as the colonization of the Amazon region, as Marcia described: "The dispute over land here in this region has always been constant, since the beginning, when the

160 Lopes de Jesus/presidenta FETAGRI-PA, Interview 2022.
161 Andrade, Interview 2022.
162 Rezende Figueira, Interview 2022.
163 Feliz and Jamiro/CPT, Interview 2022.

first Christian set his foot in the Amazon region."[164] But it seems that violence, especially against Indigenous people, increased during the Bolsonaro government,[165] and, as Mauricio Torres argued, that had to be legitimized:

> You need to have ideological legitimacy to be able to loot. So, you need to get them [the Indigenous people] out of that territory because they are backward, because they are poor, they are ugly, they don't live like people. All these in quotes. I'm just repeating the speeches of these ignorant people. Bolsonaro once reiterated that the Indians live more and more like people, or some nonsense like that.[166] This is endless racism. And this ideologically justifies, ideologically legitimizes the territorial attacks on the lands of Indigenous peoples, without a doubt.[167]

This legitimizing strategy is not only based on hatred, as it seems in the citation of the interview with Mauricio Torres, but it is also based on a kind of civilizing mission, which tries to integrate the Indigenous people into the Brazilian economy while devaluating their way of life.

Racist speeches during the Bolsonaro government were not only made against Indigenous people, but against non-white people in general; not only by the president, but also by other political leaders.[168] Regarding *trabalho escravo*, there is a clear connection to structural racism; poverty is higher among the non-white population, and the labour-

164 Marcia/CPT, Interview 2022.

165 Nádia Pontes, "Violência contra indígenas explodiu durante era Bolsonaro," Deutsche Welle, 26.07.2023, https://www.dw.com/pt-br/viol%C3%AAncia-contra-ind%C3%ADgenas-explodiu-durante-era-bolsonaro/a-66359132 [accessed 31.08.2023].

166 "'Cada vez mais, o índio é um ser humano igual a nós', diz Bolsonaro em transmissão nas redes sociais," Globo, 24.01.2020, https://g1.globo.com/politica/noticia/2020/01/24/cada-vez-mais-o-indio-e-um-ser-humano-igual-a-nos-diz-bolsonaro-em-transmissao-nas-redes-sociais.ghtml [accessed 31.08.2023].

167 Torres, Interview 2022.

168 "Autoridades públicas proferiram 94 discursos racistas durante o governo Bolsonaro, aponta levantamento," CartaCapital, 22.03.2022, https://www.cartacapital.com.br/politica/autoridades-publicas-proferiram-94-discursos-racistas-durante-o-governo-bolsonaro-aponta-levantamento/ [accessed 31.08.2023]; Franco Alves da Silva, "O racismo de Jair Bolsonaro: origens e consequências." Nexo, 18.11.2020, https://www.nexojornal.com.br/ensaio/2020/O-racismo-de-Jair-Bolsonaro-origens-e-consequ%C3%AAncias [accessed 31.08.2023].

ers doing *trabalho escravo* are recruited out of the poorest sections of society. Non-white labourers comprise 80 percent of all labourers freed from this labour condition in Brazil, while they make up 83 percent of those freed in Pará.[169] Furthermore, structural racism is also mirrored in other violations of rights, as Xavier Passat stated regarding Afro-descendants:

> We have data showing that in fact, 75 percent of *escravos* (slaves) are Afro-descendants.[170] So, that's no joke. And it is the same proportion that we find for all serious violations in Brazil. Murdering a youngster, unlawful incarceration, 75 percent [of those murdered or charged] are still black people.[171]

But the presence of non-white labourers doing *trabalho escravo* in agriculture is not only associated with class. Non-white people are especially chosen for physically straining work, as the labour inspector Carlos cleared up:

> "Sometimes they need people to work on the administrative part [...] I'm talking about [...] simple things. The salary is a little better, but they are white people. But to do the hard work, in the rural sector, they choose black people, black men, poor with low education and no income. [...] This is on purpose, Julia."[172]

And this, just like the racism against Indigenous people, is also connected to an ideology that dates back to colonial times; that is, it is connected to slavery, as the union leader Angela Conceição Lopes de Jesus explained:

169 SmartLab, "Observatório da Erradicação do Trabalho Escravo e do Tráfico de Pessoas."
170 This is different, as his numbers do not include Indigenous people and Asian descendants, for example.
171 Plassat/CPT, Interview 2022.
172 Carlos/inspetor do trabalho, Interview 2023.

> If you go to see the people who are *escravizados* (enslaved) [...], they are black or dark-skinned, there are hardly... There are white people, but the majority is black, and also due to the difficulty of their work, because they [the employers] think that black people have strength. [...] Look, I made a statement for a citrus company. [...] And it caught my attention that all the people were from the northeast, near here, in the Citropar company.[173] [...] And I asked the HR guy: 'Why do you hire labour from outside and not from Pará?' [...] 'Because look, all black men are strong. And they are very good at working, and they are very productive.' [...] This mentality is still present today; it is entrenched in the minds of the business community.[174]

In general, it is interesting to note that the views of most of my interview partners on racism changed between 2014 and 2022. In 2014, most of them said that racism had nothing or nearly nothing to do with *trabalho escravo*, and that it was more about class structure. In 2022, most of my interview partners admitted a strong intersection between racism and *trabalho escravo*. It seems that the very overt racism of the Bolsonaro government at least weakened the ideological class reductionism, which was very strong in Brazil in 2014.

Regarding gender relations, most of the rescued labourers are still men who were doing corporal labour, while most of the rescued women were working as cooks or domestic labourers, especially in agricultural enterprises. Of all the labourers rescued from *trabalho escravo* between 1995 and 2020, women made up only 5.5 percent of those labourers in Brazil and 7.6 percent of those in Pará.[175] This has to do with the reality of agricultural labour – more men than women are employed in this sector; but it also has to do with discourses about female labour in Brazilian society as well as with the practices of labour inspection building up on these discourses. In recent discussions, however, it is repeated that women doing *trabalho escravo* are also of high importance, as did, for example, the journalist Natalia Suzuki:

173 See: Citropar Agropecuária Ltda., http://citropar.com.br/contato/ [accessed 31.08.2023].
174 Lopes de Jesus/presidenta FETAGRI-PA, Interview 2022.
175 Comissão Pastoral da Terra, "Panorama atualizado do trabalho escravo no Brasil."

> On the farm, it's usually men [who work under *trabalho escravo*], but we can't forget about the women. For example, practically every time you have men, a group of men recruited, there's also a woman. There is at least one woman to do the housework, which is basically cooking. [...] We had a recent case, I think from 2017 or 2018, which was in mining. The men were mining, and the women were doing domestic service and sexual activities, and this is also *trabalho escravo*, because they were also dependent. They were in the gold mines, with accumulated debt and work activities, both sexual and domestic, mediated by a debt relationship.[176] *Trabalho escravo* also affects the female population, and this is important to be looked at, regardless of the quantity [of female labourers ...], precisely because you have an invisibility – both of women in relation to gender and in relation to the type of labour that these women do. Domestic labour in Brazil is not considered labour, for example. People are also not used to seeing sexual activities as labour, as a lucrative activity that would both generate resources and demand rights for female labourers.[177]

Today, the discourse as well as the labour inspections have started to focus more on products other than cattle, which, apart from mining, are often family-based productions and therefore also include women, and sometimes children. But also, domestic labour and, to a lesser degree, prostitution have been receiving more attention from the labour inspectorate.[178] While *trabalho escravo* in domestic labour was still "[...] completely invisible three years ago",[179] the case of Madalena Gordiano, who was freed in 2020 after living and working for forty years in that working condition, put a focus on domestic labourers. At the Fifteenth Scientific Reunion of the *Research Group on Trabalho Escravo* in Aracaju

[176] Probably this case: Instituto Chico Mendes de Conservação da Biodiversidade, "Operação resgata trabalhadores de garimpo ilegal," 23.08.2018, https://www.gov.br/icmbio/pt-br/assuntos/noticias/ultimas-noticias/operacao-resgata-trabalhadores-de-garimpo-ilegal [accessed 06.08.2024].
[177] Suzuki/Reporter Brasil, Interview 2022.
[178] Grupo RAICE, Interview 2022.
[179] Plassat/CPT, Interview 2022.

in 2022,[180] domestic labour was one of the central topics, and the labour inspectorates have since intensified their investigation into this sector. Only in the labour inspectorate of Pará is domestic labour still a branch in development.[181]

Conclusion: Global Factors and Possible Future Developments

The modalities of *trabalho escravo* and labour inspections are therefore changing and are being influenced by state politics, by the needs of the market as well as by different actors. However, it is important to keep in mind that the influences on and the consequences of *trabalho escravo* do not only unfold on a Brazilian level, but also on a global one, as journalist Natalia Suzuki stated in 2022:

> *Trabalho escravo* is not a terminally Brazilian problem; it is a transnational problem. It fits perfectly into the contemporary economy. It is not an archaic, historical remnant of a colonized country like Brazil. First-world countries, Europe, the United States – they all benefit from *trabalho escravo*. The world economy needs *trabalho escravo*. […] So, it is structural in the sense that the causes and the use of *trabalho escravo* are engendered in the contemporary economy and society, not as a remnant, but as a lucrative instrument of this economy. And it is political from the moment you do not have the political will to depose this

180 The XV Reunião Científica: Trabalho Escravo Contemporâneo e Questões Correlatas (Fifteenth Scientific Meeting: "Contemporary Slave Labour" and Related Questions) a meeting of the Grupo de Pesquisa Trabalho Escravo Contemporâneo (Research Group on "Contemporary Slave Labour"), held from November 16–18, 2022.

181 Carlos/inspetor do trabalho, Interview 2023; Plassat/CPT, Interview 2022; About the case of Madalena Gordiano see for example: Lucas Figueira, and Paulo Barbosa, "Madalena Gordiano: envolvidos no caso da mulher que viveu 40 anos em situação análoga à escravidão em MG são ouvidos em audiência," Globo, https://g1.globo.com/mg/triangulo-mineiro/noticia/2023/03/14/madalena-gordiano-envolvidos-no-caso-da-mulher-que-viveu-40-anos-em-situacao-analoga-a-escravidao-em-mg-sao-ouvidos-em-audiencia.ghtml [accessed 31.08.2023].

system. Because even politics and the economy talk to each other, and the elites are in both the economy and politics.[182]

Therefore, *trabalho escravo* is embedded in the structure of the global economy. This is also because global and local companies are in competition with each other and pursue, as far as labour relations are concerned, the same goal: the cheapest possible production, with the cheapest possible labour force.[183] *Trabalho escravo* represents, at least partly, the capitalist logic of cheap labour power, not only because of the labour regime itself, but also because with it, the wages of "free" labourers can be lowered. Furthermore, similar labour conditions also exist outside of Brazil, and Brazilian products such as orange juice, beef, dendê oil, the super fruit açai, and noble wood, for example, are subjects for export; so is gold, as most of the gold in Brazil is exported. This means that unfree labour and the products of *trabalho escravo* are all part of the global market.[184]

In addition, the fight for better working conditions in general and the abolition of *trabalho escravo* in particular take on a global scale, as social movements also have global networks. They can put pressure on the state via the global public or human rights organisations, which in turn can influence interstate relations, as could be seen in the fight to create laws against *trabalho escravo* that involved the OAS, for example.[185]

Apart from this short overview on the global dimension of *trabalho escravo*, after an introduction to the way *trabalho escravo* was formerly described to function, this article looked at the changes in the system of this working condition as well as in the politics regarding its execution. Huge changes could be detected in the sectors where *trabalho escravo*

[182] Suzuki/ Reporter Brasil, Interview 2022.

[183] David L. Levy, "Political Contestation in Global Production Networks." *The Academy of Management Review* 33, no. 4 (2008): 943–63, at 947.

[184] André Schröder, "Raids Reveal how Illegal Gold from Indigenous Lands Gets Laundered in Brazil," Mongabay, 29.08.2022, https://news.mongabay.com/2022/08/raids-reveal-how-illegal-gold-from-indigenous-lands-gets-laundered-in-brazil/ [accessed 31.08.2023].

[185] Plassat/CPT, Interview 2014.

is found, and with that, also in the system of production. Up to now, however, it remains unclear if this is because of a change in the scope of inspections or a change in the use of this labour condition. The new sensibility with respect to *trabalho escravo* in sectors other than cattle raising is also true for Pará, even though cattle still seem to be the most important product here. The most obvious changes in terms of state politics concerning *trabalho escravo* during the Bolsonaro government are the financial and personnel bloodletting of the mechanisms that were intended to fight it, as well as a discourse that propagates violence in general, one which has deep effects on the system of *trabalho escravo*.

This, of course, is only a first step in the research on the connection between the Bolsonaro (and Temer) government and *trabalho escravo*. It should be investigated more deeply, including the changes in the system itself, maybe with a critical view on the numbers that the labour inspections produce. Furthermore, recent political changes in the fight against *trabalho escravo* after the return of Luiz Inácio Lula da Silva (PT) as president in 2023 could already be studied. With his return, and given all of these power struggles inside and outside the government involving this labour regime, there could be hope for a change for the better as during his former terms as president, the mechanisms and instruments in the fight against *trabalho escravo* considerably improved. Marcia from the CPT Marabá also expressed this hope in our interview, shortly after the elections in 2022:

> We do have hope. We are holding on in any way to the possibility of change. There are changes in sight, but I still believe that this change depends on us, on each individual. We elected a president [Luiz Inácio Lula da Silva] who at least has a lot of will. Politically, he wants to do things for people in need, for the poorest people, although he will look out for all the beings that live in Brazil. He has to rule for everyone. So, he's going to have to make a lot of concessions [...] We know that it won't be easy for him to govern if he doesn't have a good political base, and if he doesn't have a good social base. And when I say social base, it is us and the people who also believe in this change who have to put

> the pressure on the government. […] So, there is hope, but this hope is very fragile.[186]

When Luiz Inácio Lula da Silva became president at the beginning of 2023, he and his government declared that they would make the environment one of their most important issues, with the Amazon region at its centre; they also announced policies in favour of Indigenous rights. In addition, they planned to revive diplomatic international relations and to implement measures benefitting the impoverished part of the population. Even though contested, their green agenda seems to have made quite considerable advances, as did the diplomatic agenda of the new government. As for the impoverished population, no impressive measures seem to have been taken yet. Also, the resources of the labour inspectorate are still too little, and the reasons why someone like Bolsonaro was voted in the first place have not disappeared either. The agro-industrial, religious, and military forces – inside and outside of classical politics – are still very strong.[187] Therefore, both Marcia's assessment of the current political situation, in that there is a need for the population to be involved, and the "fragile hope" that she expressed are quite appropriate.

---

[186] Marcia/CPT, Interview 2022.

[187] Carlos Juliano Barros, "Combate ao trabalho escravo é a principal marca dos 100 dias de Lula 3," UOL, 11.04.2023, https://economia.uol.com.br/colunas/carlos-juliano-barros/2023/04/11/combate-ao-trabalho-escravo-e-a-principal-marca-dos-100-dias-de-lula-3.htm [accessed 31.08.2023]; Leandro Prazeres, "Como meio ambiente virou aposta de Lula para aumentar influência global do Brasil," BBC, 07.08.2023, https://www.bbc.com/portuguese/articles/c1wv2nx729po [accessed 31.08.2023]; André Singer, "El regreso de Lula," *Nueva Sociedad* 305 (2023): 35–63; rfi, "Lula: o balanço do 1° ano de governo e a volta do Brasil à cena internacional," UOL, 01.01.2024, https://noticias.uol.com.br/ultimas-noticias/rfi/2024/01/01/lula-o-balanco-do-1-ano-de-governo-e-a-volta-do-brasil-a-cena-internacional.htm [accessed 15.03.2024].

Bibliography

"Autoridades públicas proferiram 94 discursos racistas durante o governo Bolsonaro, aponta levantamento," CartaCapital, 22.03.2022, https://www.cartacapital.com.br/politica/autoridades-publicas-proferiram-94-discursos-racistas-durante-o-governo-bolsonaro-aponta-levantamento/ [accessed 31.08.2023].

"Brazil is the World's Fourth Largest Grain Producer and Top Beef Exporter, Study Shows," Embrapa 50, 01.06.2021, https://www.embrapa.br/en/busca-de-noticias/-/noticia/62619259/brazil-is-the-worlds-fourth-largest-grain-producer-and-top-beef-exporter-study-shows [accessed 31.08.2024].

"'Cada vez mais, o índio é um ser humano igual a nós', diz Bolsonaro em transmissão nas redes sociais," Globo, 24.01.2020, https://g1.globo.com/politica/noticia/2020/01/24/cada-vez-mais-o-indio-e-um-ser-humano-igual-a-nos-diz-bolsonaro-em-transmissao-nas-redes-sociais.ghtml [accessed 31.08.2023].

"Ciclo do Trabalho Escravo Contemporâneo," https://escravonempensar.org.br/biblioteca/ciclo-do-trabalho-escravo-contemporaneo-2/ [accessed 07.04.2024].

"Entenda o projeto de lei da terceirização aprovado pela Câmara," Agencia Brasil, https://agenciabrasil.ebc.com.br/economia/noticia/2017-03/entenda-o-projeto-de-lei-da-terceirizacao-aprovado-pela-camara [accessed 08.08.2023].

"Jair Bolsonaro Accused of Inciting Genocide before the International Criminal Court," Open Democracy, 29.11.2019, https://www.opendemocracy.net/en/democraciaabierta/jair-bolsonaro-accused-inciting-genocide-international-criminal-court/ [accessed 30.08.2023].

"MRV," https://www.mrv.com.br/ [accessed 04.04.2024].

"Pecuária perde mais um grande nelorista e 'Rei do gado do Pará'," CompreRural, 01.03.2024, https://www.comprerural.com/pecuaria-perde-mais-um-grande-nelorista-bene-mutran/ [accessed 04.04.2024].

"Plano mais Brasil não é um projeto de crescimento, mas de aprofundamento da desigualdade econômica e social. Entrevista especial com

Guilherme Delgado," https://www.ihu.unisinos.br/categorias/159-entrevistas/594272-plano-mais-brasil-nao-e-um-projeto-de-crescimento-mas-de-aprofundamento-da-desigualdade-economica-e-social-entrevista-especial-com-guilherme-delgado?gclid=EAIaIQobChMInOzjwtGd_AIVKexcCh0thwUjEAMYASAAEgJPpPD_BwE [accessed 13.07.2023].

"Reforma trabalhista completa um ano sob questionamentos e sem desfecho," Senadonoticias, 09.09.2018, https://www12.senado.leg.br/noticias/materias/2018/11/09/reforma-trabalhista-completa-um-ano-sob-questionamentos-e-sem-desfecho [accessed 10.08.2023].

Acselrad, Henri. "A Amazônia e o antiambientalismo de resultados," Le Monde Diplomatique Brasil, 12.08.2020, https://diplomatique.org.br/a-amazonia-e-o-antiambientalismo-de-resultados/ [accessed 30.08.2023].

Alves da Silva, Franco. "O racismo de Jair Bolsonaro: origens e consequências," Nexo, 18.11.2020, https://www.nexojornal.com.br/ensaio/2020/O-racismo-de-Jair-Bolsonaro-origens-e-consequ%C3%AAncias [accessed 31.08.2023].

Andrade, Jônatas. Interview by Julia Harnoncourt, 30.10.2014, Marabá.

Andrade, Jônatas. Interview by Julia Harnoncourt, 28.10.2022, webex.

Andreas and Maria/MST. Interview by Julia Harnoncourt, 01.11.2014, Acampamento Hugo Chavez, Pará.

Angelo, Mauricio. "Trabalho escravo em garimpos expõe redes criminosas na Amazônia," Mongabay, 11.02.2021, https://brasil.mongabay.com/2021/02/trabalho-escravo-em-garimpos-expoe-redes-criminosas-na-amazonia/ [accessed 12.08.2023].

Antonho/Secretaria Municipal de Agricultura Tucumã. Interview by Julia Harnoncourt, 23.11.2014, Tucumã.

Bansal, Vaiddehi, Jessica Wallach, Juliana Lira Brandão, Sarah Lord, Ninar Taha, Tulay Akoglu, Ligia Kiss and Cathy Zimmerman. "An Intervention-Focused Review of Modern Slave Labor in Brazil's Mining Sector," *World Development* 171, no. 70 (2023).

Barros, Carlos Juliano. "Conquista da Fazenda Cabaceiras: Escravidão temporária, luta de classes e reforma agráriano sul do Pará," *Anais Encontro Nacional dos Geógrafos* 16 (2010).

Barros, Carlos Juliano. "O sonho se faz a mão e sem permissão: "Escravidão temporânea" e reforma agraria no sudeste do Pará"(PhD diss., Universidade de São Paulo, 2011).

Barros, Carlos Juliano. "Combate ao trabalho escravo é a principal marca dos 100 dias de Lula 3," UOL, 11.04.2023, https://economia.uol.com.br/colunas/carlos-juliano-barros/2023/04/11/combate-ao-trabalho-escravo-e-a-principal-marca-dos-100-dias-de-lula-3.htm [accessed 31.08.2023].

Boadle, Anthony, and Lisandra Paraguassu. "Satellite Data Shows Amazon Deforestation Rising under Brazil's Bolsonaro," Reuters, 04.06.2019, https://www.reuters.com/article/us-brazil-environment-deforestation-idUSKCN1T52OQ [accessed 30.08.2023].

Brass, Tom. *Labor Regime Change in the Twenty-First Century: Unfreedom, Capitalism and Primitive Accumulation* (Chicago: Haymarket, 2013)

Brexior Pereira, Antonio, and Jarbas Henrique Sampaio Azevedo. "Formulário de denúncia de trabalho escravo," 20.06.2008, CPT Xinguara.

Brito, Ricardo, and Gabriel Araujo. "Bolsonaro Barred from Holding Public Office in Brazil until 2030," Reuters, 01.06.2023, https://www.reuters.com/world/americas/political-career-brazils-bolsonaro-dangles-by-thread-electoral-trial-nears-end-2023-06-30/ [accessed 08.08.2023].

Buzatto, Gleber César. "O governo Bolsonaro e o anticonstitucionalismo contra os povos indígenas," Le Monde Diplomatique Brasil, 22.01.2019, https://diplomatique.org.br/o-governo-bolsonaro-e-o-anti-constitucionalismo-contra-os-povos-indigenas/ [accessed 13.07.2023].

Camargos, Daniel. "Após 7 flagrantes, MRV é beneficiada por acordo com governo e fica fora da 'lista suja' do trabalho escravo," Repórter Brasil, 28.10.2022, https://reporterbrasil.org.br/2022/10/apos-7-flagrantes-mrv-e-beneficiada-por-acordo-com-governo-e-fica-fora-da-lista-suja-do-trabalho-escravo/ [accessed 30.08.2023].

Carlos/inspetor do trabalho. Interview by Julia Harnoncourt, 10.01.2023, webex.

Carstensen, Anne Lisa. *Das Dispositiv moderne Sklavenarbeit: Umkämpfte Arbeitsverhältnisse in Brasilien*, International Labour Studies 23 (Frankfurt: Campus Verlag, 2019).
Carstensen, Lisa. "Trabalho Forçado e Tráfico de Pessoas: Uma Análise do Discurso em Instituições e Organizações Internacionais e Brasileiras," *Brasiliana. Journal of Brazilian Studies* 2, no. 2 (2013): 3–31.
Carstensen, Lisa. "Unfree Labour, Migration and Racism: Towards an Analytical Framework," *Global Labour Journal* 12, no. 1 (2021).
Carstensen, Lisa. "Flexibilisierung und Prekarisierung von Arbeit in globalen Produktionsketten – informelle Heimarbeit in der Bekleidungsindustrie in Puebla und São Paulo," Sozial.Geschichte Online 13 (2014): 7–40, http://duepublico.uni-duisburg-essen.de/servlets/DocumentServlet?id=34889 [accessed 05.08.2024].
Carstensen, Lisa, and Shioban McGrath. "The National Pact to Eradicate Slave Labour in Brazil: A Useful Tool for Unions?" *The National Labour Column* 117 (2012).
CDVDH/CB and CPT. *Por debaixo da Floresta: Amazonia paraense saqueada com trabalho escravo* (São Paulo: Urutu-Branco, 2017).
Centro de Documentação Dom Tomás Balduino, ed. "Conflitos no Campo: Brasil 2022," Goiânia, 2023.
Citropar Agropecuária Ltda. http://citropar.com.br/contato/ [accessed 31.08.2023].
Comissão Pastoral da Terra. "Panorama atualizado do trabalho escravo no Brasil: coleção e análise de dados" [accessed 26.08.2023, sent via email 30.06.2022].
Cowie, Sam. "A bordo de uma balsa de garimpo: quanto vale a vida no mercado de ouro ilegal?" Repórter Brasil, 13.09.2021, https://reporterbrasil.org.br/2021/09/a-bordo-de-uma-balsa-de-garimpo-quanto-vale-a-vida-no-mercado-de-ouro-ilegal/ [accessed 16.08.2023].
Da Silva Farias, Leandro. "Formulário de denúncia de trabalho escravo," CPT Xinguara.
Davey-Attlee, Florence. "Brazil's Bolsonaro Accused of Crimes against Humanity at ICC for His Record on the Amazon," CNN, 12.10.2021, https://edition.cnn.com/2021/10/12/americas/brazil-bolsonaro-icc-crimes-against-humanity-intl/index.html [accessed 30.08.2023].

De Amada Conceição, Luís Fernando. "Declaração July 17, 2014," CPT Tucumã.
De Castro Gomes, Ângela Maria. "Repression and Changes in Slave-Like Labor in Brazil: In the Present time and Uses of the Past," *Revista Brasileira de História* 32, no. 64 (2012): 151–67.
De Oliveira, Cida. "MST foi decisivo em desapropriação de terras com trabalho escravo, diz pesquisa," Rede Brasil Atual, 12.03.2012, http://www.redebrasilatual.com.br/cidadania/2012/03/mst-foi-decisivo-em-desapropriacao-de-fazenda-com-trabalho-escravo-aponta-estudo-da-usp [accessed 28.08.2023].
De Souza Martins, José. "The Reappearance of Slavery and the Reproduction of Capital on the Brazilian Frontier," in *Free and Unfree Labour: The Debate Continues*, ed. Tom Brass and Marcel van der Linden (Bern: Lang, 1997): 281–302.
Do Nascimento Pereira, Raimundo Nonato, and Francisco Almeida Rodriguez. "Formulário de denúncia de trabalho escravo," CPT Xinguara.
Estreci, Neide. *Escravos da desigualdade: Um estudo dobre o uso repressivo da força de trabalho hoje* (Rio de Janeiro: Centro Edelstein de Pesquisas Sociais, 2008).
Feliz and Jamiro/CPT. Interview by Julia Harnoncourt, 09.11.2022, Tucuruí.
FGV. "R$ – Renda Média da População – UF," https://cps.fgv.br/r-renda-media-da-populacao-uf-2020 [accessed 03.03.2024].
Figueira, Lucas, and Paulo Barbosa. "Madalena Gordiano: envolvidos no caso da mulher que viveu 40 anos em situação análoga à escravidão em MG são ouvidos em audiência," Globo, https://g1.globo.com/mg/triangulo-mineiro/noticia/2023/03/14/madalena-gordiano-envolvidos-no-caso-da-mulher-que-viveu-40-anos-em-situacao-analoga-a-escravidao-em-mg-sao-ouvidos-em-audiencia.ghtml [accessed 31.08.2023].
Fiscalía. "Resumo da ação fiscal," 2008, Archive CPT Xinguara.
Governamento Brasil, "PRF em Operação Conjunta com o Ministério Público do Trabalho atua no Combate ao Trabalho Escravo," https://www.gov.br/prf/pt-br/noticias/estaduais/goias/2022/novem-

bro/prf-em-operacao-conjunta-com-o-ministerio-publico-do-trabalho-atua-no-combate-ao-trabalho-escravo [accessed 23.02.2024].
Grupo RAICE. Interview by Julia Harnoncourt, 10.11.2022, Itupiranga.
Harnoncourt, Julia. “Trabalho escravo? Ein historischer Vergleich auf globaler Ebene,” *JahrBuch für Forschungen zur Geschichte der Arbeiterbewegung* 14, no. 3 (2015): 63–77.
Harnoncourt, Julia. *Unfreie Arbeit: Trabalho escravo in der brasilianischen Landwirtschaft,* Edition Kritische Forschung (Wien: Promedia, 2018).
Harnoncourt, Julia, and Miguel Paredes. “Theorizing Human Trafficking and Unfree Labor,” *Journal of Global South Studies* 40, no. 1 (2023): 173–212.
Hauchere Vuong, Aurélie. “A Multidisciplinary Approach to Combat Forced Labour – Lessons Learned from Brazil,” *Global Eye on Human Trafficking* 12 (2013).
Hegenberg, Ivan, “Aspectos subjectivos de nossa crise política,” Le Monde Diplomatique Brasil, 02.10.2015, https://diplomatique.org.br/aspectos-subjetivos-de-nossa-crise-politica/ [accessed 30.08.2023].
Iana/CPT. Interview by Julia Harnoncourt, 22.10.2014, Xinguara.
Instituto Chico Mendes de Conservação da Biodiversidade, “Operação resgata trabalhadores de garimpo ilegal,” 23.08.2018, https://www.gov.br/icmbio/pt-br/assuntos/noticias/ultimas-noticias/operacao-resgata-trabalhadores-de-garimpo-ilegal [accessed 06.08.2024].
Johnson, Maya. “$200 Million in Gold Extracted in Amazon Mine through Illegal Licenses,” Mongabay, 25.10.2021, https://news.mongabay.com/2021/10/200-million-in-gold-extracted-in-amazon-mine-through-illegal-licenses/ [accessed 31.08.2023].
Konchinski, Vinicius, “Brasil usa mais agrotóxicos que Estados Unidos e China juntos,” *Brasil de Fato*, 05.02.2024, https://www.brasildefato.com.br/2024/02/05/brasil-usa-mais-agrotoxicos-que-estados-unidos-e-china-juntos [accessed 04.04.2024].
Le Breton, Binka. *Vidas roubadas: A escravidão moderna na Amazônia Brasileira* (São Paulo: Loyola, 2002).
Levy, David L. “Political Contestation in Global Production Networks,” *The Academy of Management Review* 33, no. 4 (2008): 943–63.

Lopes de Jesus, Angela Conceição/presidenta FETAGRI-PA. Interview by Julia Harnoncourt, 04.11.2022, Belem.

Luana/CPT. Interview by Julia Harnoncourt, 20.11.2014, Tucumã.

Maranhão Costa, Patricía T. “Fighting Forced Labour: The Example of Brazil,” Special Action Programme to Combat Forced Labour, Geneva, 2009.

Marcia/CPT. Interview by Julia Harnoncourt, 10.11.2022, Marabá.

Martig, Alexis. “Slaving Zones, Contemporary Slavery and Citizenship: Reflections from the Brazilian Case,” in *Slaving Zones: Cultural Identities, Ideologies, and Institutions in the Evolution of Global Slavery*, ed. Jeff Fynn-Paul and Damian A. Pargas (Leiden: Brill, 2018): 336–59.

Máximo, Welton. “Brasil resgatou 3,1 mil trabalhadores escravizados em 2023: Apesar de falta de fiscais, essa é a maior marca anual desde 2009,” Agencia Brasil, 03.01.2024, https://agenciabrasil.ebc.com.br/direitos-humanos/noticia/2024-01/brasil-resgatou-31-mil-trabalhadores-escravizados-em-2023 [accessed 09.02.2024].

McGrath, Shioban, and Kendra Strauss. “Unfreedom and Workers' Power: Ever-Present Possibilities,” in *Handbook of the International Political Economy of Production*, ed. Kees van der Pijl (Cheltenham: Edward Elgar, 2015): 299–317.

Mendes Moreira Miraglia, Lívia, Julianna do Nascimento Hernandez and Rayhanna Fernandes de Souza Oliveira, eds. *Trabalho Escravo Contemporâneo: Conceituação, desafi os e perspectivas* (Rio de Janeiro: Lumen Juris, 2018).

Ministèrio de Trabalho e Emprego. “Combate ao Trabalho em Condições Análogas às de Escravo,” https://www.gov.br/trabalho-e-emprego/pt-br/assuntos/inspecao-do-trabalho/areas-de-atuacao/combate-ao-trabalho-escravo-e-analogo-ao-de-escravo [accessed 16.03.2024].

Molina, Luísa, and Luiz Jardim Wanderley. *O cerco do ouro: garimpo ilegal, destruição e luta em terras Munduruku* (Brasilia: Comitê Nacional em Defesa dos Territórios Frente à Mineração, 2021).

Motoki, Carolina, Brígida Rocha dos Santos and Waldeci Campos de Souza. “De 1995 a 2022: o trabalho escravo contemporâneo a partir dos dados sistematizados pela Comissão Pastoral da Terra,” in “Conflitos no Campo: Brasil 2022,” Goiânia, 2023: 141–61.

Neves, Julia, "Carteira de trabalho verde e amarela: entenda seu funcionamento," oitchau, 28.06.2023, https://www.oitchau.com.br/blog/carteira-de-trabalho-verde-e-amarela-entenda-seu-funcionamento/ [accessed 30.08.2023].

Organização Internacional do Trabalho. *Perfil dos principais atores envolvidos no trabalho escravo rural no Brasil* (Brasilia: OIT, 2011).

Padre Paulinho/CPT. Interview by Julia Harnoncourt, 11.11.2014, Belém.

Penha, Daniela, and Diego Junqueira. "Aposta de Lula contra a fome, reforma agrária continua parada após 2 meses de governo," MST, 15.03.2023, https://mst.org.br/2023/03/15/aposta-de-lula-contra-a-fome-reforma-agraria-continua-parada-apos-2-meses-de-governo/ [accessed 04.04.2024].

Perez, Fabiola. "Ações do PCC fortalecem permanência de garimpeiros na Terra Yanomami," UOL, 03.05.2023, https://noticias.uol.com.br/cotidiano/ultimas-noticias/2023/05/03/pcc-acao-garimpeiros-terra-indigena-yanomami.htm [accessed 31.08.2023].

Pina, Rute. "No Brasil, 2 mil latifúndios ocupam área maior que 4 milhões de propriedades rurais," Brasil de Fato, 26.06.2018, https://www.brasildefato.com.br/2018/07/26/no-brasil-2-mil-latifundios-ocupam-area-maior-que-4-milhoes-de-propriedades-rurais [accessed 03.03.2024].

Plassat, Xavier /CPT. Interview by Julia Harnoncourt, 26.11.2014, Araguaína.

Plassat, Xavier /CPT. Interview by Julia Harnoncourt, 07.11.2022, Araguaína.

Pontes, Nádia. "Violência contra indígenas explodiu durante era Bolsonaro," Deutsche Welle, 26.07.2023, https://www.dw.com/pt-br/viol%C3%AAncia-contra-ind%C3%ADgenas-explodiu-durante-era-bolsonaro/a-66359132 [accessed 31.08.2023].

Portela de-Assis, Mariana, Raquel Cristine Barcella, Janaína Chiogna Padilha, Hildegard Hedwig Pohl and Suzane Beatriz Frantz Krug. "Health Problems in Agricultural Workers Occupationally Exposed to Pesticides," *Revista brasileira de medicina do trabalho publicação oficial da Associacao Nacional de Medicina do Trabalho-ANAMT* 18, no. 3 (2021): 352–63.

Prazeres, Leandro. “Como meio ambiente virou aposta de Lula para aumentar influência global do Brasil,” BBC, 07.08.2023, https://www.bbc.com/portuguese/articles/c1wv2nx729po [accessed 31.08.2023].

Ramos, Mauro. “Pará: Sem terra relatam noite do atentado contra o acampamento Hugo Chávez,” Brasil de Fato, 16.08.2018,” https://www.brasildefato.com.br/2018/08/16/para-sem-terra-relatam-noite-do-atentado-contra-o-acampamento-hugo-chavez [accessed 30.08.2023].

Rezende Figueira, Ricardo. *Pisando fora da própria sombra: A escravidão por dívida no Brasil contemporâneo* (Rio de Janeiro: Civilização Brasileira, 2004).

Rezende Figueira, Ricardo. “A Persistência da Escravidão Ilegal no Brasil,” in *Desafios aos Direitos Humanos no Brasil Contemporâneo*, ed. Brion Maybury-Lewis and Sonia Ranincheski (Brasília: Verbena, 2011): 49–64.

Rezende Figueira, Ricardo. Interview by Julia Harnoncourt, 17.11.2022, Aracajú.

Rezende Figueira, Ricardo, Adonia Antunes Prado and Rafael Franca Palmeira. “L’esclavage contemporain et ses transformations en Amazonie brésilienne: Les témoignages des victimes,” *Brésil(s)* 11 (2017).

Rezende Figueira, Ricardo, Adonia Antunes Prado and Edna M. Galvão, eds. *Trabalho Escravo Contemporâneo: Estudos sobre ações e atores* (Rio de Janeiro: Mauad X, 2017).

rfi. “Lula: o balanço do 1° ano de governo e a volta do Brasil à cena internacional,” UOL, 01.01.2024, https://noticias.uol.com.br/ultimas-noticias/rfi/2024/01/01/lula-o-balanco-do-1-ano-de-governo-e-a-volta-do-brasil-a-cena-internacional.htm [accessed 15.03.2024].

Russau, Christian, “Sklavenarbeit auf der VW-Fazenda Rio Cristalino in Amazonien,” https://www.kooperation-brasilien.org/de/themen/menschenrechte-gesellschaft/sklavenarbeit-auf-der-vw-fazenda-rio-cristalino-in-amazonien [accessed 11.07.2023].

Sadia. https://www.sadia.com.br/ [accessed 31.08.2023].

Sakamoto, Leonardo. “Perfil de uma família escravocrata,” *Observatorio Social* 2004, no. 6: 28–32.

Sakamoto, Leonardo, and Renato Bignami. *Escravidão contemporânea* (São Paulo: Editora Contexto, 2020).

Schröder, André. “Raids Reveal how Illegal Gold from Indigenous Lands Gets Laundered in Brazil,” Mongabay, 29.08.2022, https://news.mongabay.com/2022/08/raids-reveal-how-illegal-gold-from-indigenous-lands-gets-laundered-in-brazil/ [accessed 31.08.2023].

Singer, André. “El regreso de Lula,” *Nueva Sociedad* 305 (2023): 35–63.

SmartLab. “Observatório da Erradicação do Trabalho Escravo e do Tráfico de Pessoas,” https://smartlabbr.org/trabalhoescravo/ [accessed 09.02.2024].

Southey, Flora. “More Trees, Less Land: How Brazil’s Orange Juice Sector Trippled Its Productivity,” FoodNavigator, 09.10.2022, https://www.foodnavigator.com/Article/2022/12/09/Densification-How-Brazil-s-orange-juice-sector-produces-more-with-less [accessed 31.08.2023].

Suzuki, Natália. Interview by Julia Harnoncourt, 18.08.2022, Zoom.

Thays/CDVDH. Interview by Julia Harnoncourt, 26.11.2014, Araguaína.

Torres, Mauricio. Interview by Julia Harnoncourt, 20.12.2022, Whatsapp.

Walk Free. “The Global Slavery Index 2023,” https://www.walkfree.org/global-slavery-index/downloads/ [accessed 26.08.2023].

Zé, Dudu. “Marabá: juiz Jônatas Andrade irá receber Prêmio Direitos Humanos 2012 das mãos da presidente Dilma,” 06.12.2012. http://www.zedudu.com.br/?p=26837 [accessed 27.08.2023].

For further titles see: www.ebverlag.de

EBVERLAG DR. BRANDT WWW·EBVERLAG·DE

Rainer Kuhl
Jägerstraße 47
13595 Berlin

Tel.: 00 49 30 68 97 72 33
Fax: 00 49 30 91 60 77 74
E-Mail: post@ebverlag.de